"*Bonding with Your Child through Bo*⸻ ⸻ ⸻ ⸻ ⸻ ⸻ vith solid, biblical advice on the situations paren⸻ ⸻ ⸻ ⸻ ⸻ u're struggling with your kids over tem⸻ ⸻ ⸻ ⸻ ⸻ ⸻ g, or even if you're just looking for w⸻ ⸻ ⸻ ⸻ ⸻ se, this book has something for you."

> **Jim Daly**, President, Fo⸻

"If children are a part of your l⸻ ⸻ ⸻ ow hold in your hands the *real* answers to the *real* challenges you face. Each practical chapter spells out 'What you could do' and 'What you could say'—not to win a war, but to win a *relationship* of respect. *Bonding with Your Child through Boundaries* encourages every parent to build a positive connection with their kids through wisdom, grace, and responsibility."

> **Karol Ladd**, Founder, Positive Life Principles; author, *The Power of a Positive Mom*

"Every parent who holds biblical principles sacred MUST read *Bonding with Your Child through Boundaries*. Not only is this practical book grounded in God's Word, it's born out of real-life struggles. Don't miss out on this immensely practical message."

> **Les and Leslie Parrott**, Founders, Center for Relationship Development, #1 NYT Authors, *The Parent You Want to Be*

"From back talk and bullying . . . to temper tantrums and bedtime battles, June presents parent-tested ideas that really work for real challenges as verified by coauthor and mother of seven, PeggySue Wells. If you have children in your life, you will be grateful for this valuable parenting guide."

> **Catherine Hart Weber**, Director, Flourish in Life and Relationships Center for Wellbeing; author, *Flourish: Discover Vibrant Living*

"Once again, June has captured the attention and the hearts of parents! What parent hasn't cried out, at least internally, for help to rein in their children? What parent hasn't prayed for help to lovingly guide sons and daughters in the way of the Lord? Well-respected and loved for her *Biblical Counseling Keys* for life's issues, June provides the guidance parents are seeking to set healthy boundaries while bonding with their most precious gifts from God."

> **Carmen Pate**, Principal, Communications, Alliance Ministries and The 210 Project

"Parents today face an increasingly complex task in raising children in a fast-paced world full of digital distractions while immersed in a post-Christian culture. This book will serve as a wonderful resource for parents to strengthen their bond with their child through boundaries."

> **Daniel Egeler**, President, Association of Christian Schools International

"As a guidance counselor in a Christian school, I'll refer to *Bonding with Your Child through Boundaries* constantly in my work with students, parents, and teachers—just as I've done for years with June's companion book for teens. June's biblical, practical approach is evident on every page. It's an indispensable resource for every Christian school administrator, counselor, and teacher."

Angela Paxton, Guidance Counselor, Legacy Christian Academy, Frisco, Texas

"Never has this book been more needed than now and no one is more perfect for handling the responsibility than June Hunt. June's ministry provides a background for understanding why children need boundaries to grow into healthy, productive adults. This resource is refreshing and full of helpful insights."

Janice Shaw Crouse, Management Committee, World Congress of Families; author, *Children at Risk* and *Marriage Matters*

"Just as football—or any other sport—needs boundaries and rules to make it fun and interesting, children need boundaries to feel secure and confident. June's book makes this plain in a powerful way, with lots of great action points to help you put boundaries into practice with your kids. These insights are important—not only for us, but for our entire culture, and the next generation of parents and children."

Carey Casey, CEO, National Center for Fathering

Bonding with
Your Child through
Boundaries

Bonding with Your Child through Boundaries

June Hunt

with PEGGYSUE WELLS

WHEATON, ILLINOIS

Library of Congress Cataloging-in-Publication Data
Hunt, June.
Bonding with your child through boundaries / June Hunt, with PeggySue Wells.
    pages cm.
Includes bibliographical references.
    ISBN 978-1-4335-4334-0 (tp)
    1. Parent and child—Religious aspects—Christianity. 2. Child rearing—Religious aspects—Christianity. 3. Parenting—Religious aspects—Christianity. I. Title.
BV4529.H85   2015
248.8'45—dc23   2015000586

To my niece Kathryn,
the most exceptional mother I know.

Kathryn is always the first to
redirect praise for her parenting back to God . . .
and to the other women who have spoken into her life.

- Women like her Granny Ruth, who always invited Kathryn to kneel beside the bed with her . . . so they could talk with the Lord together. Today, Kathryn devotes daily time to praying with her own children because she views prayer as a precious privilege.
- Then there's her mother, Helen, who taught Kathryn, when she was little, to make decisions for herself . . . to avoid being too dependent on others. Likewise, Kathryn again and again allows her children opportunities to become great decision makers!
- And of course, her kids' "Aunt Kimmy" is a consistent encourager . . . assuring them all, "You are unconditionally loved by your family . . . and by your Lord."

Some would say educating six children at home isn't the most promising path for a bright, capable PhD—one who is sought after by universities to speak and teach. Yet long ago, Kathryn chose not to have a splintered life, but rather a boundaried life in which she would "do one thing well."

She chose to say *no* to other paths so she might say *yes* to God's path. She dedicates her time, talent, and treasure to be the best wife and mother possible—a decision she's never regretted.

Kathryn guards her time and invests it intentionally, modeling a life devoted to God and family. In so doing, she instills that same intentionality in her young ones. Her genuine relationship with Jesus . . . her unwavering focus on holiness . . . her prayerful reverence for God . . . permeates every aspect of her life.

She strategically plans her days with character-building projects . . . often cleverly disguised as "family fun." Just as God's boundaries have become hers, they increasingly become her kids' as well. And as a result, her grateful children—ranging in age from one to fourteen—"stand and bless her" (Prov. 31: 28 TLB).

Today my genuine joy is to "stand and bless" this extraordinary mother and mentor . . . and especially now *a remarkable mentor to other young mothers.*

Contents

Acknowledgments

This book is the product of dozens of committed Christians who contributed ideas, research, writing, editing, proofing, critiquing, and other forms of indispensable expertise—all for a common goal: to help parents train up future generations of godly children.

Though space prohibits me from detailing your generous contributions, I am keenly aware of them and, of much greater comfort and consequence, so is *God*!

My friends . . .

Angela Paxton

Angie White

Barbara Spruill

Bea Garner

Beth Funk

Carolyn White

Elizabeth Cunningham

Jill Prohaska

Jody Capehart

Julia Camarigg

June Page

Karen Billman

Karen Stebbins

Karen Williams

Kathryn Rombs

Kathy Hughes

Kay Yates

Peggy (Karra) Schaffer

PeggySue Wells

Phillip Bleecker

Sheila Brown

Steve Hunter

Steve Murphy

Tara Davis

Titus O'Bryant

Trudie Jackson

Vallene Hendrix

. . . may God bless and richly reward your diligent work, done in his name and for his glory.

> "We give thanks to God always for all of you, constantly mentioning you in our prayers, remembering before our God and Father your work of faith and labor of love and steadfastness of hope in our Lord Jesus Christ."
>
> (1 Thess. 1:2–3)

Introduction

A Personal Word to Parents

Oh, the joy of little ones in our lives! Hearing gurgling giggles from chubby cheeks. Smiling at tongue twisters lisped through missing teeth. Seeing tiny tots run on tippy toes, plopping down on padded bottoms, then snuggling close for bedtime stories. Is there anything cuter than a freshly bathed cherub in footed pajamas? Not on this side of heaven!

Parenting is one of life's greatest privileges—one of God's highest callings. The Bible tells us, "Children are a gift from the LORD" (Ps. 127:3 NLT), and those with a full house are indeed blessed. Realize, *your children are your personal, God-given priority, your closest and most enduring "mission field."*

Yet, over the years I've seen so many parents perplexed—and too many parents in pain. Well-meaning parents say, "Just tell me what to do, June—I promise I'll do it!" But the answer isn't a simple, one-step "it." The answer is a mind-set that seems to work miracles. This life-changing mind-set is centered on the word *boundaries* and flanked between two *R*s—*repercussions* and *rewards*.

When I was a youth director in my twenties, I saw dismayed parents who obviously had never heard of *boundaries*, or at least had never learned how to use them. They had no concept of how boundaries could be a relationship lifesaver—so helpful for both parents and kids. That is the "why" of this book.

Raising respectful, self-disciplined children is such an important assignment that the apostle Paul even makes it a litmus test for those seeking church leadership (see Titus 1:6; 1 Tim. 3:4). The inference is clear: If parents can't lead their own children, who on earth *can* they lead? But what about godly parents who practice God's principles and follow in his footsteps, yet have children who are bent on rebellion? Thankfully, the Bible offers encouragement.

Even God, the Perfect Parent, suffers heartbreak over his rebellious children—and not for lack of wisdom. Think about the very first boundary on earth: As a perfectly wise and loving Father, he provides the ideal home for his first son and daughter. And as good parents do, he communicates boundaries to help his children clearly understand what is expected of them—what constitutes right behavior. He also explains the repercussion for crossing over the boundary saying, "You may freely eat the fruit of every tree in the garden—except the tree of the knowledge of good and evil. If you eat its fruit, you are sure to die" (Gen. 2:16–17 NLT).

Then God does something that has puzzled people ever since—he gives his children . . . *choice*. Now equipped with "free will," Adam and Eve can stay within their Father's boundaries and receive a reward (the ability to live with him in Paradise for all eternity). Or they can violate his boundary and reap numerous repercussions (eviction from their home, loss of intimacy with their Father, and painful hardship in their lives—not to mention death).

At the moment Adam and Eve willfully choose to disobey, the very first parental boundary is crossed. And, soon, the first repercussion is enacted. Ever since then, effective parents have been using boundaries (with rewards and repercussions) to bring up their children "with the discipline and instruction that comes from the Lord" (Eph. 6:4 NLT).

And that, my friend, is precisely the point of this book. Created to be the "prequel" to *Bonding with Your Teen through Boundaries*, this companion volume combines *biblical hope* and *practical help* for parents of grade-school children, including tweens (ages nine through twelve), and even children as young as two or three.

In fact, this book was conceived as a direct response to parents who, after reading our *Teen* book, said, "June, we desperately needed a book like this when our kids were younger!"

As with the *Teen* book, section 1 explains the essential role of boundaries, gives general principles for implementing the best boundaries, and answers the most frequently asked questions about boundaries. The thirty-six short chapters in section 2 provide practical, parent-tested "how-to" steps for making boundaries work in *your* family, with *your* child. Many of the scenarios come from real parents with real challenges—parents who have called my live two-hour call-in counseling broadcast, HOPE IN THE NIGHT, desperate to know *God's Truth for Today's Problems.*

Featured in each of these thirty-six chapters is a real-life scenario, followed by practical "What You Could Do" and "What You Could Say" sections to help take much of the guesswork out of implementing boundaries. Each chapter ends with a related verse from the Bible to encourage your heart and impart Scripture to your children.

The parent-child relationship rests on the careful balance of loving affirmation and loving discipline. All the affection in the world cannot substitute for godly discipline. Nor can discipline be a substitute for tender affection. Don't confuse one with the other. Kids depend on their parents to supply both, just as we look to our heavenly Father to supply both.

Parenting is the most demanding, rewarding, faith-building job most people will ever undertake. I sincerely thank you for the privilege of coming alongside you on a journey designed to improve the life of your child . . . and also a journey that could very well change *your* life.

My sincere prayer is that you lovingly bond with the Lord through the boundaries laid out in his Word so that you will gain the wisdom needed to *bond with your child through boundaries.*

Yours in the Lord's hope,

June

P.S. As I did in the *Teen* book, I sometimes use the word *kids* to refer to children. Years ago when I was a youth director, I often talked about "my kids" as a term of endearment. For those strict grammarians to whom *kid* will only mean "young goat," I hope you will indulge me. (No kidding!)

Section 1

What Are Boundaries All About?

"We hope that your faith will grow so that the boundaries of our work among you will be extended."

(2 Cor. 10:5 NLT)

More than Ever, Your
Child Needs Boundaries

Parenting has always been one of life's toughest jobs. But in recent years, the task has grown even more challenging. Gone are the days when most families gather for church *together*, then share Sunday dinner *together*; when parents always know where their children are; when parents aren't worried about their kids because everyone looks out for each other's kids.

Today's children are being hijacked by a culture that hurls them into adulthood prematurely. From media to mainstream, the message is "Grow up!" Afternoons spent playing hopscotch and hide-and-seek have been replaced with countless extracurricular activities and media mania. Schools that once served as positive laboratories for learning are increasingly filled with negative first-hand learning . . . about drugs, gangs, and sexual experimentation.

Therefore, equipping kids to be deeply self-disciplined (and consistently respectful) and to prioritize principle over passion requires enormous wisdom, motivation, and commitment—as well as faith and hard work. In order to help you help them, never has it been more important to nurture a close relationship with your child, a one-on-one relationship of respect and two-way trust through *boundaries*.

What Are Boundaries?

Boundaries are *established limits*—lines not to be crossed.[1] Even very young children understand boundaries. Bathrooms have doors. Cribs have sides. Streets have curbs.

In most areas of life, when a boundary is exceeded, the result is a *repercussion*. And most often, when a boundary is maintained, the result is a *reward*.

Picture an Olympic arena with all the white lines on the racetrack. Hear the blast of the start gun. See the runners burst out of the blocks. Watch as one sprinter darts into another runner's lane and hear the crowd gasp. The *repercussion* is instant—immediate disqualification. What a horrible way to lose! Yet, as long as the others stay inside their own lanes, the *reward* of finishing is theirs— along with the possibility of winning.

Realize, almost every sport has boundaries. They are absolutely necessary. And if those boundary lines were removed, what you would see is a free-for-all!

Behaviors have boundaries too. Whether boundaries are ethical, moral, legal, or biblical, they all distinguish *right from wrong*. Sometimes legal boundaries overlap with moral, ethical, and biblical boundaries, as in the case of theft. In the Ten Commandments, God states, "You shall not steal" (Ex. 20:15). Stealing is wrong on every level. Thus, those who are caught can expect hefty repercussions.

Why Do Kids Need Boundaries?

External boundaries are designed to develop internal character. Read these words again. This statement is the most important concept in this book. Boundaries are not about *you* getting your kids to do what *you* want them to do.

Kids who live without boundaries—without right repercussions and rewards—feel frustrated, insecure, and confused by the inevitable lack of order in their lives. Ultimately, parents who let their kids keep getting away with wrong are *training* them to *do wrong*.

Conversely, when kids consistently experience appropriate repercussions for breaking a boundary, those negative consequences provide *predictable pain*. In turn, that pain motivates kids to develop discipline in order to prevent future pain.

Realize, *doing right* eventually *feels right*. Kids with character do the right things—not to impress the world, but because they've been transformed by a powerful process described in Romans 12:2: "Do not be conformed to this world, but be transformed by the renewal of your mind, that by testing you may discern what is the will of God, what is good and acceptable and perfect."

President Franklin Roosevelt said, "We cannot always build the future for our youth, but we can build our youth for the future."[2] To face that future, children need to master numerous milestones, including being able to accept delayed gratification, motivate themselves, persist against frustration, empathize with others, and control their impulses.[3] Beneficial boundaries equip kids to succeed in these areas.

Boundaries also help stem the tide of *self-centered entitlement* that threatens to engulf our culture—a tide that urges children to worship at the altar of *New—More—Now*. They feel entitled to have what they want. "I *deserve* new! I *deserve* more! I *deserve* now!" Child psychologist Dr. James Dobson correctly reveals that few things inhibit a "sense of appreciation more than for a child to feel he is entitled to whatever he wants, whenever he wants it."[4]

As caring adults, we also establish boundaries to address our children's three basic inner needs: love, significance, and security.[5] While only Christ can meet these needs completely, parents lay the spiritual and emotional groundwork by maintaining healthy boundaries at home. These boundaries will provide stability for what otherwise would be an unstable foundation and will create a family "culture of accountability."[6]

Consider the findings of a fascinating sociological study where young children played in a large, open field. With no fences or boundaries, the children huddled rather closely together, playing fearfully. Conversely, when the children were observed in a large field bounded by tall fencing on all sides, they wandered to the far corners of the field and played with greater confidence.[7]

This experiment illustrates a timeless truth: children instinctively *search* to locate their limits. Adults often misinterpret this search as a dislike for limits, whereas exactly the opposite is true. Kids keep pushing their parents—testing their limits—until they find boundaries that do not change. Once they discover fair, unchangeable limits, they *feel secure* within those limits. They feel safe and can relax . . . and ultimately, *so can you.*

Many boundaries come equipped with built-in repercussions and rewards—consequences that impart memorable lessons. *"If you forget to take your homework to school, you'll get a zero." "It's freezing outside! If you refuse to wear your coat at the game, you'll feel bitterly cold."* It's important to allow your child to experience *natural outcomes* whenever possible. These painful lessons can retrain the brain and build Christlike character.

Allow children to *practice making choices* and to experience natural rewards or repercussions. These consequences will prepare them for the adult world, which is ordered by boundaries . . . from making payments on time (to avoid financial penalties) to meeting deadlines on time (to avoid being fired).

How Are Boundaries Best Implemented?

Implement boundaries in *reverse proportion* to your children's maturity. When they are youngest and most defenseless, kids need parental boundaries at every turn. When you base these boundaries on biblical principles, you train your children to respect God's authority in their lives, along with the boundaries.

The more children mature, the fewer parent-imposed boundaries they need. Then when they enter adulthood, you fully release them, praying the biblical boundaries they learned at home will serve them for a lifetime.

Boundaries presented in positive terms are effective teaching tools to help your child avoid frustration, failure, and danger. Especially when dealing with young children, express boundaries in terms of what *to* do and what *is* expected, rather than what *not* to do and what will *not* be tolerated.

Instead of saying, "Don't open the door without knocking," give positive instruction, such as, "When a door is closed, knock before entering." Change "Don't tip back in your chair," to "Keep all four legs of your chair on the floor."

As you establish boundaries, do you want your kids' respect? Consider this significant statement: "With children, more is *caught* than *taught*." Do *you* always:

- Tell the truth when it's inconvenient?
- Observe the speed limit?
- Spend your money wisely?
- Control your temper? Your weight?
- Ask forgiveness when you're wrong?

Children have a built-in antenna for authenticity. As a positive, proactive parent, it's vital to model staying within the boundaries—not only for your children's sake, but also as a matter of integrity before God.

Be assured: You will either respect boundaries yourself and train your kids to respect them too, or your kids will train you when they realize that *they* will decide whether to obey you or not.

Count on them to test your resolve: Will you accept excuses for bad behavior? Turn a blind eye or a deaf ear? Talk tough, but fail to act?

Initially, it's not evil or wrong for your kids to test boundaries. That's normal! That's their job. (Testing is different from rebellious defiance.) Children learn by testing boundaries to ensure they are secure. But when they test, your job is to *be ready* and lovingly *hold firm*. This book will help you do both.

Your unwillingness to excuse poor behavior communicates confidence in your child. It says, "I believe you are capable of doing what is right. You have it in you to display self-control. And I love you enough to accept nothing less."

When children are secure in who they are—and *whose* they are—they are better equipped to make good decisions. The Bible says, "Discipline your children, and they will give you peace of mind and will make your heart glad" (Prov. 29:17 NLT). In short, *boundaries can be a parent's most powerful parenting tool.*

Checkpoint

Is your child enjoying life and laughing regularly? Are you? A natural consequence of establishing boundaries is reduced stress. Boundaries create space for joy between you and your child.

2

What Color Is Your Hat?

In old-time Western movies, it didn't take long to discover who was the *good guy* and who was the *bad guy*. The good guy always wore a white hat, and the bad guy always wore a black hat. Everyone liked the hero in the white hat. No one liked the villain in the black hat.

Who Wants to Wear the Black Hat?

And so it goes in the family. Every parent wants to be liked and respected and, of course, no parent wants to be the villain. So what do you do when your children deliberately disobey—and you don't want to be perceived as a villain wearing "the black hat"?

Some parents assume the solution is *permissiveness*: Allow kids to do whatever they want (often against a parent's better judgment) so the kids won't get upset and the family can live in peace. For kids who cross the line: no reprimand, no reproach, and no repercussion.

But this passive peace-at-any-price approach won't reap the positive results you desire. You want to raise a self-disciplined child who respects your role as a parent and your right to set the rules.

What Color Is *Your* Hat?

Not certain if you are a peace-at-any-price parent? Take this quiz and find out.

- Do you avoid confronting your child's negative behavior?
- Do you fail to discuss uncomfortable situations with your child?
- Do you give in easily to your child's whining or tantrums?
- Do you cover up or make excuses for your child's bad behavior?
- Do you continually extend "another chance" without establishing or enforcing consequences?
- Do you repeatedly rescue your child from natural consequences caused by negative behavior?
- Do you fail to consistently implement rules and boundaries?
- Do you withhold discipline in fear of losing your child's love?

If you answered yes to any of these questions, you are not alone. The good news is that there is a better way . . . by bonding with your child through boundaries.

Wasn't Jesus a Peace-at-Any-Price Person?

Many people—Christians and non-Christians alike—think peace at any price is the Christian way to live. *After all*, they reason, *Jesus is called the Prince of Peace*. They quote Jesus's words: "My peace I give to you" (John 14:27); "Blessed are the peacemakers" (Matt. 5:9). The apostle Paul even said, "If possible, so far as it depends on you, live peaceably with all" (Rom. 12:18).

In light of these biblical passages, we need to ask ourselves, *Was Jesus a peace-at-any-price person?* The answer is: absolutely *not*! Instead, he countered this common misconception by pronouncing, "I have not come to bring peace, but a sword" (Matt. 10:34). Jesus clearly communicated that we must confront what is wrong, getting to the heart of the matter. He proclaimed, "And you will know the truth, and the truth will set you free" (John 8:32).

The sword of truth, which is the Word of God, is necessary to live a life of integrity and to confront needed changes when nothing around you is peaceful. If you do what is right in his sight, Jesus gives you his supernatural peace—an internal "peace of God, which surpasses all understanding" (Phil. 4:7).

He is the Prince of Peace (Isa. 9:6). *He will be your peace* in the midst of any storm—even a stormy time with your child. But having the peace of Christ on the inside is entirely different from being a peace-at-all-costs parent.

What Happens When You Are a Peace-at-Any-Price Parent?

We've all encountered the results of permissive parenting—at the store, in the doctor's office, on the playground. Without boundaries, kids control their parents. If these kids don't get their way, they can act out *dramatically*. The peace-at-any-price parent quickly appeases the child by giving in to disruptive behavior. Through their manipulative tactics, children learn that, with enough crying, screaming, and boisterous clamor, they'll bulldoze through mommy or daddy's "no." Thus, the family perpetually remains one tantrum away from chaos.

Peace-at-any-price parents fear public embarrassment and being disliked by their children. Ironically, abdicating their parental role is the surest way to bring about these very outcomes. Undisciplined children will grow to:

1. *Disrespect* appropriate rules
2. *Dismiss* the need for self-discipline
3. *Disregard* authority
4. *Despise* their parents
5. *Dishonor* biblical commands
6. *Disown* personal responsibility

Conversely, when parents establish clear boundaries—with appropriate repercussions and rewards—the child is given *the choice* to stay within the boundary or not. And here's the parents' most freeing part: This means *the child*, not the parent, is the one who *chooses the repercussion* or *the reward*! This also means you no longer wear the black hat! This empowers the child to make good choices based on logical consequences. Parents also benefit because consistent boundaries make a portion of the disciplinary process automatic.

Implementing fair and firm boundaries will equip your children for a lifetime of learning, achievement, service, and moral purity. Initially, will they consider you to be the bad guy wearing the black hat? Probably. But I can tell you, based on more than thirty years of counseling/life coaching experience and the many promises in God's Word: one day, you will see your black hat turn white.[1]

Checkpoint

Does the thought of upholding boundaries make you fearful? What are you most afraid of? Write it down, then ask the Lord to replace your weakness and fear with faith in his strength to empower you to stand firm. "When I am afraid, I put my trust in you" (Ps. 56:3).

3

The Confident Parent

God intended "home" to be an incubator for children, a place for kids to explore their world and to become all he created them to be. Within this safe nest, your role is to nurture their potential, discourage their defiance, and focus on their strengths.

Scripture tells us, "Train up a child in the way he should go; even when he is old he will not depart from it" (Prov. 22:6). This verse doesn't mean there is one ironclad set of boundaries appropriate for training all children or that parents who adhere to those rules are guaranteed godly offspring.

The point of parenting is not to cultivate uniform perfection. "Train up a child in the way he should go" refers to understanding the natural bent of each of your children and encouraging their growth from that perspective.

Quite literally, you embark on a divine treasure hunt, searching for the strengths God has sovereignly hardwired into your children. How? Introduce them to a variety of experiences and topics and then watch closely to see where their interests and abilities lie. As you discern their God-given strengths, you need to establish firm and fair boundaries to instill the self-discipline required to reach their full potential.

On my live two-hour call-in counseling program, *HOPE IN THE NIGHT*, I often refer to the importance of changing "minds, hearts, and lives." I order the words this way intentionally, to reflect the actual progression of how people grow and change. Your goal as a parent, then, is to help shape the minds and hearts of your children—cultivating inner attitudes that will be reflected in their outer behavior—for a lifetime.

What Are Important Dos and Don'ts of Discipline?

In addition to the tips listed in chapter 2, consider these important dos and don'ts for bonding with your child through boundaries.[1]

Do . . . mold your children's will without breaking their spirit. That old saying is true: "Rules without relationship lead to rebellion."[2] Even as you reinforce boundaries, treat children with kindness, patience, fairness, and respect. This will uplift their spirit, demonstrating their value as a unique creation of God. Children need their parents to lovingly affirm them with plenty of hugs, kisses, and pats on the back. They need you to praise their efforts—which they can control—not just their abilities.

Don't . . . use harmful practices such as unfairness and harsh punishment, impatience and jumping to conclusions, perfectionism and hurtful comparisons, or other tactics that constitute verbal or emotional abuse.[3] To avoid humiliating your child, support in public, confront in private.

Consider a wild stallion. Every horse has intrinsic value; however, the most valuable stallion turns with the slightest nudge from the rider's reins. The master's goal is to shape (or "break") the horse's will, without breaking its spirit. A parent's goal is to shape the will of the child without breaking the spirit. The Bible says, "Fathers, do not provoke your children, lest they become discouraged" (Col. 3:21).

Do . . . communicate your expectations clearly. Model effective communication. Prior to problems arising, describe in detail what you expect your children to do (and not to do) and what will result regarding rewards and repercussions.

When training your children to obey, you'll sometimes need to give gentle reminders. Mastering new information doesn't happen overnight. After all, it even takes adults twenty-one days to form a habit.

However, I don't recommend habitually "counting to three" before expecting your child to do what you've told him to do. A countdown can encourage your child to wait until "three" and delay to obey! God's best for our lives occurs when we obey his "still small voice" the first time we hear it (1 Kings 19:12 NKJV). Likewise, children will benefit by learning to obey the very first time.

Don't . . . plead, excuse, lecture, or become emotionally distraught when your child disobeys. These tactics remove the focus from the problem behavior and place it on . . . *you*. Speak clearly and confidently and, if necessary, rehearse or role-play your words before they're spoken. Don't allow your children to negotiate and argue with you as if they were your peers. *They're not*.

Some families create a written list of House Rules that are discussed with each child to ensure understanding and then posted in a visible location. House Rules enable you to refer children (old enough to read) to a tangible document—an ever-present reminder of what is expected in your home. For ideas, consider the House Rules posted on the refrigerator of my conscientious niece Kathryn, a phenomenal mother of six.

- Obey Mom and Dad. Say "Yes, Mom" or "Yes, Dad" to let them know I understand.
- Look at adults when they talk to me.
- When I want something, ask, "May I please have _____?" (See also "Sharing" on p. 212 for more on this topic.)
- Put away what I use when I'm finished.
- No whining, yelling, pouting, or grumbling. Ask kindly for what I want.
- Tell the truth and do it with love. No name-calling, teasing, or hurtful words.
- Use my outside voice outside and my inside voice inside.
- Put dirty clothes in the hamper.

- Morning routine is: breakfast, get dressed, brush hair and teeth, make bed, and clean room.
- No interrupting. Stop, look, and listen. If someone is speaking, say, "Excuse me," one time. Then wait until they turn to me.
- When I get a gift, look the person in the eye, smile, and clearly say, "Thank you."
- Call someone "Sir" or "Ma'am" if they're grown-ups.
- Seats on the seats. No climbing on furniture.
- Keep my hands to myself during church. (Coloring quietly is okay.)

Do . . . wisely pick your "battles," leaving room for kids to act like kids. Don't be overly rigid, bound by rules, or legalistic. However, when your kids cross established boundaries, enact firm and fair repercussions—every time. Said another way: Wise parents pick their battles, and *win* the battles they pick. Never underestimate your children's awareness that they are breaking the rules. Therefore, never excuse or tolerate *willful violations* of important boundaries.

Don't . . . punish children for acting their age—when they're not being rebellious. The point of parenting is not perfection. Allow and encourage children to express themselves—their questions, doubts, fears, and skepticism—with creativity and youthful exuberance.

I still remember being in a grocery store with my mother and seeing a two-year-old tyke riding in the child's seat of a grocery cart. He reached out his short arm and toppled down five cereal boxes from the big display. The mother started yelling and berating the little boy, who began to cry buckets of tears.

"What a shame," my mother exclaimed. "He was just doing what two-year-olds do—he saw bright red and yellow boxes and wanted to touch them. She could have corrected him without harshly criticizing him."

Do . . . help your children see their misbehavior as a problem *they* **can solve.** This teaches them problem-solving skills that will serve them for a lifetime and helps them own their behavior rather than excuse it. When you identify misbehavior as a "problem" and ask your children what they plan to do about their problem, you communicate that *they*, not you, need to take a leading role in finding a solution.[4]

For example, if your son misses the school bus, you could say, "Getting up in time to catch the bus seems to be a problem for you. What do you think you should do about that? Let's come up with some things you can do to get to the bus on time. I'd like to hear your ideas." (Getting to bed earlier and preparing clothes/lunches/backpacks/homework the night before are a few options that would involve your child in the problem-solving process.)

Don't . . . allow your children to transfer their problems to you. Yes, you want to be available to help. But, whenever possible, *don't let your child's problem be your problem! Don't rescue kids from the repercussions of their own responsibilities.* Allowing kids to reap repercussions based on their problem behavior reinforces this point. We are individually responsible for our own irresponsibility. "So then each of us will give an account of himself to God" (Rom. 14:12).

What Is the Difference between Helping and Rescuing?

Well-intended, caring parents may think they're helping their children when, in reality, they're hurting them. What is the difference? When parents "rescue" them from reaping their deserved repercussions, they circumvent the purpose of boundaries. These parents don't understand that their children's struggle to gain self-control and discipline builds character, strength, and confidence.

Galatians 6:2 says, "Bear one another's burdens, and so fulfill the law of Christ." The Greek word for *burden* is *baros*, which means "weight," implying a load or something that is pressing heavily. When you help carry something too heavy for someone alone to bear, your helpfulness fulfills the law of Christ.

Galatians 6:5 (just three verses later) states, "For each will have to bear his own load." The Greek word here for *load* is *phortion*, which means "something carried." Clearly, when you carry what someone else should carry, you are unwise. Thus, you are not called by God to relieve your children of their rightful responsibilities . . . and repercussions.

Certainly at times you should come alongside with compassion and walk beside a hurting child through a difficult situation. However, *be careful not to rescue them from being responsible.*

For example, teaching your young children to make their bed is *helping*. Making the bed for your complaining nine-year-old is needlessly *rescuing*. Coaching a child through the steps required to be on time for a Saturday T-ball game is *helping*. Arguing with a coach who benches your child for repeatedly being late is *rescuing*.

Rescuing your children from doing distasteful tasks silently conveys, "Others are able to do this task but I know you can't because you're deficient," or "You're too special or too good to do things you don't want to do." By doing this, you deny them the opportunity to achieve their full potential. Likewise, rescuing children from deserved repercussions that ultimately serve their best interest trains them to see themselves as helpless victims of anyone who might find fault with them.

How do you avoid falling into the rescuing trap?

- Focus on being your children's parent-trainer, not their parent-buddy.
- Hold your children personally accountable when they are at fault. If they get in trouble, don't automatically blame someone else.
- If your children don't complete school assignments, resist doing the task for them.

How Can You Make the Most of Teachable Moments?

Skilled parents watch for their children's readiness to learn various new skills at specific times in their growth and development. Child development experts call these times of heightened receptivity "teachable moments."

For example, children who insist on performing a difficult task themselves may need several opportunities to fail before being open to their parent's guidance. Sometimes the failure itself opens their hearts, showing them their need for instruction. These valuable moments are times when wise parents put aside whatever else they may be doing to focus on teaching their children.

Kids are constantly learning how their world works. During teachable moments, welcome their questions. Help them recognize their options. When your kids present an idea, enlist their feedback in your response. Ask questions like: "Could you think of ways to make that happen?" "What do you think would happen if you tried that?" "If you could do it differently, what would you do?" These kinds of questions help them think through cause and effect—an important skill in constructing healthy boundaries of their own.

To capitalize on their readiness to learn, become an active student of your children. Genuinely listen to what they say. Observe what fills their hearts with excitement. Celebrate the rewards that come their way and help them to discover the repercussions of crossing a boundary. Teachable moments that are seized create a childhood filled with growth and opportunity.

Of course, the most important teachable moment your children could ever have is the moment they see their need for Jesus to be their Lord and Savior. Watch prayerfully for this opportunity and, when it arrives, be ready to introduce them to an authentic relationship with Jesus Christ. You will find a sample script on "How to Lead Your Child to Christ" in the Appendix. This, along with other resources on child evangelism, available through HOPE FOR THE HEART, will help you prepare for what may be the most pivotal experience of your child's life.

How Can You Simultaneously Correct and Affirm?[5]

Children hunger to know they are valued and loved. When you say, "I'm proud of you," you speak life-giving words into their hearts. Yet kids often need to be corrected, even rebuked.

How can you correct kids without crushing their tender spirits? Can you encourage an attitude change while keeping the lines of communication open—and keeping real issues as the main focus? For decades, I've recommended a powerful technique—included in my *Biblical Counseling Keys* on "Parenting"—called the Sandwich Technique.[6] Not only do I personally use it to confront and correct behavior, I have taught countless parents to do likewise.

To begin, imagine a sandwich with three layers. Each layer represents a step in the confrontation process.

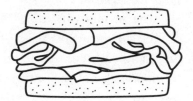

Bread of Appreciation

Meat of the Matter

Bread of Encouragement

1. Begin with the "Bread of Appreciation." Sincerely praise an internal character trait (not physical appearance or talents).

   Example: "All that skateboard practice is paying off. You're working so hard to improve and it shows!"

   Proverbs 16:24 says, "Gracious words are like a honeycomb, sweetness to the soul and health to the body."

2. Now add the "Meat of the Matter" by stating the problem. Recount the chain of events that led to the present problem. Examine what went wrong and why. Using questions, brainstorm options to correct the problem. Clarify the desired behavior change and determine a course of action for going forward.

   Example: "I notice you chose to leave your skateboard in the driveway instead of putting it away in the garage. If you choose not to bring it in before dinner, you'll also be choosing not to use it for the rest of the weekend."

   Proverbs 12:1 says, "Whoever loves discipline loves knowledge, but whoever hates correction is stupid" (NIV).

3. Finish with the "Bread of Encouragement"—a statement that expresses your belief that your child can make the right choice or that the future can be better than the past.

   Example: "I know you can choose to put your skateboard away after you finish riding it. I've seen you do that before, and I know you can do it again."

   First Thessalonians 5:11 says, "Therefore encourage one another and build one another up, just as you are doing."

In every chapter in section 2, you will see a segment titled "What Could You Say?" By incorporating the Sandwich Technique when you correct your child, you increase the probability that your words will be well-received.

Your time, prayers, and unconditional love are three of the greatest gifts you can give your children. In the midst of busy schedules, children will thrive on knowing they are a vitally important part of your day. Ensure they often hear the words, "You matter to me. I'm praying for you. I love you." The strongest boundary against disrespectful attitudes and actions is love! Love does what's best on behalf of another person—thus boundaries (not rescuing) is one of the most powerful expressions of love.

Checkpoint

Post a photo of a caterpillar on your bathroom mirror to remind you of this timeless truth: A caterpillar only becomes a butterfly when allowed to struggle against the boundaries of its cocoon. The struggle strengthens its fragile, developing wings. "Rescuing" the caterpillar from its boundaries—relieving the caterpillar of the struggle—will result in the death of the butterfly. It will languish and die. Hebrews 10:36 says, "For you have need of endurance, so that when you have done the will of God you may receive what is promised." *

---

* Additional resources to help you "do the will of God" as a parent are available from Hope For The Heart. These include training manuals called *Biblical Counseling Keys* on topics such as "Parenting" and "Boundaries" (http://www.hopefortheheart.org/).

Your R & R Toolkit

When it comes to childrearing, if you think R & R stands for *rest and relaxation*, you've got another *think* coming! Consider *rewards* and *repercussions* from Kathryn's point of view.

Training up children is clearly a creative calling for my niece, a mother of six who just happens to have the most well-adjusted, well-behaved kids I've ever seen. As a committed Christian with a PhD in philosophy, Kathryn homeschools her young "chicks"— currently ranging in ages from one to fourteen.

When Kathryn and her husband, Ron, are out with their kids, it's not uncommon for complete strangers to make comments like: "Your children are *so* respectful . . . *so* obedient . . . *so* polite."

As I worked on the concepts for this book, Kathryn shared with me the system of rewards and repercussions she and Ron use to cultivate a "love of obedience" in their children. Candidly, when I first heard her use this phrase, I was astonished. I'd never heard the *love of obedience* before.

That's when I realized that my mind-set regarding obedience has been more the "law of obedience"—something I *must* do, not something I love to do. Then I remembered the words of Jesus: "If you love me, obey my commandments" (John 14:15 NLT).

Obviously, I still have much to learn from my niece. In the process, I am reminded why her children are truly exceptional: *exceptional parenting!* And their system works—beautifully.

Tangibly Reward Progress

Starting when the children are as young as two, Kathryn begins "catching them doing things right" and immediately provides a tangible reward.[1] In her home, the reward is a small token.

The children collect their tokens in a plastic bag with their name on it. When they do something right—something difficult for them to accomplish—the children receive a token. If they disobey, a token is taken away. Once they accumulate ten tokens, they can trade them in for a reward. This could be a date with one of their parents, an ice cream cone, some money to spend at a store, or something especially meaningful to that particular child.

"Tokens aren't given for skills or behaviors already mastered," Kathryn explains. "Instead, they are used as motivation to help the children grow and change." For example, if a child is struggling with timeliness, Kathryn might say, "If you are on time for school five days in a row, you'll earn five tokens—one for each morning you succeed."

They tailor this technique to help their children learn almost every new skill—from putting the towel back on the rack after a bath, to chewing and swallowing food before speaking at the dinner table, to waiting patiently for a turn in a game.

As the children get older, they must earn fifteen to twenty tokens before they can receive a reward. The older children sometimes save their tokens and ask for the cash equivalent (about fifty cents each) in lieu of the reward. In fact, Jacob, the eldest, once saved tokens for an entire year so he could cash them in to buy a quality set of baseball cards.

As rewarding as it is to give and receive tokens, it's sometimes necessary to remove them. "When we witness unacceptable behavior, we remind the children that they've reached what we call 'the fork in the road,'" Kathryn explains. "We suggest they think long and hard about what they do next because *continued* poor behavior will result in the immediate loss of a token. Often, this warning is enough to correct the undesirable attitude or activity on the spot."

Touched by an Angel

Kathryn and Ron built a sweet twist into their rewards system: *Angel Activities.* "We explain, God is pleased when we obey him and serve others selflessly—for no other reason than putting a smile on his face. Activities done solely to make God smile are called *Angel Activities.*

"For example, Mary decided she wanted to make Claire's bed for her. (This doesn't normally happen!) Typically, I might give Mary a token for going out of her way to help her sister. But Mary told me she wanted to make the bed as an Angel Activity in order to make God smile, and that's exactly how we handled it. Angel Activities remind our kids that the best rewards of all are those we'll receive in heaven" (Matt. 6:19–20).

Token Alternatives

I have other friends who use similar rewards systems and report equally encouraging results. PeggySue, mother of seven, used beans in a jar instead of tokens in a bag to provide incentives for desired behaviors. Her children earned a certain number of beans each time they demonstrated the new behavior. The beans were deposited into a jar and after a week of sustained improvement, the family made bean soup and celebrated with a family game, an ice cream treat, a movie night, a picnic in the park, a lunch at the lake, a visit to the zoo, or another fun activity.

"Some of my older children chose to receive money," Peggy-Sue says. "So I'd give them fifty cents for each book read or five dollars for finishing a big project. We didn't pay them for everything. We'd all still clean the barn and mow the yard—without payment—because these responsibilities represent the privilege of being a member of the family. But when we'd finish big family projects, we'd celebrate—with hot fudge sundaes!"

Some parents fill a jar with folded slips of paper. Each one lists a reward for a week's worth of activities—such as doing chores without being reminded, completing schoolwork, vacuuming the car, completing a book, or mastering a piano piece. Rewards include foot rubs, tea parties, bubble baths, special desserts, a fun movie, later bedtimes, outings with a parent, a day off from chores, even choosing the dinner menu or choosing the game on family game night. The list of reward options keeps expanding depending on the age of each child and their preferences.

What Virtues Are You Cultivating?

To acknowledge good behavior and cultivate character, my creative niece designed a "Virtue Flower" for each child, displayed on the entry wall of the kitchen. Earlier, Kathryn bought large, colorful sheets of construction paper and then directed her kids to glue on precut paper flower stems and circles (representing the centers of the flowers). Then the kids cut out petals—a different color for each child—with the older ones helping the younger ones.

To explain the concept of virtue, Kathryn used herself as an example: "Tell me the types of actions you see me doing well . . . most all the time. Not like cooking or solving math problems, but what describes *who I am* as a person." One by one, the children began calling out answers:

- "You hug me when I'm sad."
- "You forgive me when I'm sorry for doing something wrong."
- "You let us get a puppy, and you help take care of him."

Afterward, Kathryn offers one word—a specific virtue—to describe each behavior: compassionate . . . forgiving . . . helpful . . .

Then the children took turns naming virtues they had observed in each other. Kathryn recalls, "It was so gratifying to hear them praise the positive traits of their siblings—all on their own."

"She helps me clean my part of the room." (*Thoughtful*)

"She wakes up in a good mood." (*Cheerful*)

"He lets me play with his toys." (*Generous*)

And on it goes. As virtues are identified for each child, each trait is written on a separate petal and glued to encircle the center of that child's flower.

Next comes more brainstorming: What does each child need to work on to become more like Jesus? "As you'd expect, the kids are very clear about areas where the others need improvement!" It seems *patience, obedience, truth-telling, follow-through*, and other virtues fill the list.

Every item in the "needs work" category is also written on a paper petal. But instead of being glued around the center of the flowers, the petals are merely taped lower down on the Virtue Flower's stem. Kathryn explains, "Over the weeks and months, as each child increasingly demonstrates the trait listed on the petals, we move the petals higher on the stem.

"For example, if one child isn't particularly gentle but begins to demonstrate the virtue of *gentleness*, we move the 'gentleness petal' up the stem each time we see this trait in action. Once it's an ingrained character trait, *gentleness* gets glued onto the flower. Whenever we break out the glue in our home, it's time for a big family party!"

The Give and Take of Relationship

Recently, a pastor asked a room full of parents for a show of hands: "How many of you have ever been asked by one of your children: '*What can I do to help you?*'" Spontaneous laughter erupted throughout the room. Not a single hand was raised.

Being asked such a question would dumbfound most parents—but not Kathryn. In fact, her kids quite regularly ask her—and each other—"What can I do to help you?"

Make no mistake—Kathryn's children weren't born with a rare "service gene." She explains what led to the breakthrough behavior:

"It was a day when everything began spiraling out of control at precisely the same moment. While dispensing medicine to one sick child . . . a plate slid out of my other hand, shattering into a million pieces on the floor . . . as the dryer buzzed incessantly for attention . . . and another child tugged on my pant leg, seeking clean leotards for dance practice *right now*!

"At that moment, I did what any capable, experienced, level-headed mother would do: I had a *complete meltdown*! Bursting into tears, I cried out, 'Lord! Please help me!' And that's when it dawned on me. *Why can't my children help each other*? Inspired by the possibilities, I prayerfully set out to train them to do just that.

"To begin, I explained how Jesus said in Acts 20:35, 'It is more blessed to give than to receive.' Then, I started encouraging my children to offer to help me and each other. Change didn't happen overnight, of course, but I watched for training opportunities. When I'd spot them taking the initiative to help out, I'd recognize their efforts. Sometimes, I'd also reward them with a kiss . . . not just a peck on the cheek, but the sweet chocolate kind, too.

"Now, my kids eagerly look for ways to serve each other and me. It's part of our family's culture, reinforced by the knowledge that 'God is not unjust; he will not forget your work and the love you have shown him as you have helped his people and continue to help them' (Heb. 6:10 NIV)."

Choosing Right Repercussions

You will find that each of the thirty-six topical "how-to" chapters in this book begins with a scenario where one little lamb has "gone astray" (Isa. 53:6) followed by suggestions of what to do and say when your child "crosses the line." Each "What You Could Do" section offers ideas for age-appropriate repercussions—from loss of privileges and toys, to time-outs and restrictions, to natural and physical consequences.

As with rewards, when selecting repercussions, you must factor in your child's temperament. Some children need only to see sorrowful disappointment on your face, and they become regrettably repentant. Others will better learn to obey by being placed in time-out for a brief period—a loss of freedom.

Whenever possible, make repercussions *task-oriented*, not just *time-oriented*:

- *Time-oriented repercussions* could include restricting kids to their bedroom after school for three days. But like prison incarceration, this kind of repercussion can teach kids how to "do time" versus how to change their behavior over time.
- *Task-oriented repercussions* involve kids in tasks specifically selected for them to *learn something*, to think about the impact of their behavior and their need to change. For example, if your daughter is unkind to her little sister, you could restrict her favorite activity until she writes her sister a sincere apology. The task of writing in tandem with restrictions is more effective than simply restricting her to her room—a repercussion that has nothing to do with the boundary she violated.[2]

What about the Repercussion of Spanking?

Now we've come to a highly controversial topic. Few issues ignite the passions of parents more quickly than debating the pros and cons of spanking. Both sides could present biblical principles, their own parents' practices, and a multitude of opinions to "prove" the rightness of their position.

Those who oppose spanking often offer specific objections, including:

- Spanking focuses on external compliance and short-term behavior modification rather than on internal heart attitude and long-term character transformation.
- Spanking gives a parent an unhealthy sense of power and a child an unhealthy sense of powerlessness.
- Spanking is under the law of the Old Testament, but today it contradicts the New Testament teaching on parenting.

It's true, spanking a child isn't explicitly mentioned in the New Testament. However, loving, godly discipline is: "For the Lord disciplines the one he loves . . ." (Heb. 12:6). That verse is quoting the Old Testament verse Proverbs 3:12. Ultimately, *the goal of discipline* is to shape the child's will, encourage repentance, and cultivate Christlike character (Prov. 20:11).

Even within the two opposite camps, some will say, "I'll never ever spank my child—I love my child *too much to do it!*" No matter the argument, everyone believes they are right.

If You Believe Spanking Is Biblical, What Else Do You Need to Know?

Much of the debate over spanking stems from *how* it is administered. There is a vast difference between angrily hitting or beating and calmly administering a spanking. Keep in mind that spanking *is not* a beating, *not* done in anger, *not* uncontrolled, *not* applied anywhere other than the bottom, and *not* administered by a parent who cannot remain calm.

Spanking should be applied only as a repercussion for *willful acts of disobedience*—and then only when motivated by love for your child. Proverbs 13:24 says, "Whoever spares the rod hates his son, but he who loves him is diligent to discipline him." Spanking can be the most effective, appropriate, and compassionate form of discipline.

Proverbs 23:13 says, "Do not withhold discipline from a child; if you strike him with a rod, he will not die." Another Proverb reminds parents, "Folly is bound up in the heart of a child, but the rod of discipline drives it far from him" (Prov. 22:15).

Ask the Lord for discernment in making decisions regarding disciplining your child. Pray for wisdom—the Lord promises to provide generously (James 1:5). If you decide to use spanking, consider the following practical steps.

Before spanking the first time, decide what constitutes a "spankable" offense. Spanking should be reserved only for *willful* defiance, *deliberate* disobedience—never for childish accidents (spilling the milk, breaking the plate). As the old saying goes, make absolutely sure the "punishment fits the crime."

Next, communicate this guidance to your child. You could say, "My choice would be never to give you a spanking. However, if you choose to break certain rules, then *you* are *choosing* to receive a spanking. These attitudes and actions could warrant a spanking." Then detail offenses on your list, which should be short.

After you explain the boundaries, ask your child to repeat each one back to you. Listen for understanding and ensure your child is old enough to grasp the *meaning* behind the words. Invite and answer any questions.

The first time your see that your child is about to commit a spankable offense, give a verbal warning. This provides an opportunity to change course and a reminder that there will be accountability for actions. The Bible says, "The rod and reproof give wisdom, but a child left to himself brings shame to his mother" (Prov. 29:15).

If your child commits an offense on the list, act as soon as possible so that the boundary violation will be associated with the spanking. You may want to say, "Go to your room now and think about your actions."

Once you've calmly and prayerfully collected your thoughts, here are a few "next steps" you could follow:

(1) When you are not angry, sit next to or across from your child. Begin by asking, "What did you do?" Allow your child to verbalize what was done, admitting actions. ("I lied to you.") "What is the repercussion when you choose to lie?" ("I get a spanking.") This question conditions your child to be aware that *choices have consequences*. Soon your child will begin to understand that there is a code of morality (right and wrong actions) based on God's design.

Avoid asking, "Why did you do that?" The common response to this question is, "I don't know" or a litany of excuses.

(2) You want your children to identify your hands with nurture and affection. Therefore, rather than using your hand to spank—or

a belt you wear—use a wooden spoon, paddle, or another neutral object appropriate for your child's size. A slender wooden spoon will not inflict harm on a young child, particularly because it should be applied only to the child's bottom, and in a limited measure. Two or three swats to the bottom, forceful enough to feel—but not to break or bruise the skin—is sufficient.

(3) A spanking effectively delivers sensory consequences that convey "Doing something wrong can hurt others—and *me personally.*" As you spank, be aware that children usually cry, though some will not. Don't make it a point to spank with the intent of spanking until your child cries.

After the spanking, gather your child close. After a few minutes, crying should subside. If the tears and outcry continue longer than you would expect (more than five minutes) and especially if you hear that the cries are no longer natural but forced (to manipulate your emotions), gently yet firmly say, "It's time to stop crying now."

Then ask, "Can you tell me why [name the offense] is wrong?" If the answer is correct, listen while your child explains. Add any additional points needed to help your child fully understand the repercussions of the wrong actions and the resulting ripple effects—in relationship with God and others, and on your child's heart.

(4) Conclude your time with prayer. First, you pray aloud, then encourage your child to do likewise.

Dear Lord, Thank you for letting us know what is right and what is wrong. Thank you for forgiving us when we've done wrong and for giving us the power to do right. We pray that our hearts would want what is right in your sight and that we would both yield our will to your will. Thank you for loving us and thank you that we will never be without your love. In your holy name, we pray. Amen.

"Then I acknowledged my sin to you
    and did not cover up my iniquity.
I said, "I will confess

> my transgressions to the Lord."
> And you forgave
> the guilt of my sin. (Ps. 32:5 NIV)

As with the Sandwich Technique (p. 36), remind your child of your love and of God's promises. "'For I know the plans I have for you,' declares the LORD, 'plans to prosper you and not to harm you, plans to give you hope and a future'" (Jer. 29:11 NIV).

Frequently Asked Questions about Spanking

Q: At what age is spanking appropriate?

A: From around age two until six or seven, spanking can serve as an appropriate response to *deliberate, rebellious disobedience*. Once a child reaches the transitional years of ten to twelve, use other forms of discipline.[3]

Q: Who should be allowed to spank my child?

A: A child should be spanked only by parents, not by siblings. Occasionally, you may authorize a grandparent or other caretaker to administer a spanking under specific circumstances. In some states, school officials have the authority to spank children. In these cases, you should be informed before a spanking occurs.

Q: Where should a spanking be administered?

A: Honor the dignity of your child by moving to a private place to talk about the disobedience and to administer discipline. Even in your own home, don't spank a child in front of others. Discipline won't be effective if it embarrasses or humiliates your child, nor will the Lord be honored.

Q: How often do I spank?

A: The frequency depends on your child. Training a child's heart is a battle of the will. Just because your child repeats a behavior after a spanking doesn't mean this discipline isn't effective. Learning comes through repetition, and some children require successive and consistent correction, while others respond more quickly. The Bible reminds us, "For the moment all discipline seems painful rather than pleasant, but later it yields the peaceful fruit of righteousness to those who have been trained by it" (Heb. 12:11).

Q: Does spanking perpetuate hitting and violence?
A: No. On the contrary, *if administered appropriately*, spanking can be an effective deterrent. Because spanking is not done in anger and does not involve your hand coming directly into contact with your child, it is not the same as hitting and certainly is not violent. Nor, if done correctly, does spanking perpetuate violence.

Q: What is the difference between beating and spanking?
A: Beatings are carried out in anger and continue past the point of shaping the child's will (which is the legitimate goal of spanking). Beatings result in crushing the child's spirit, which is *always wrong*. Beating is *about the aggressor*—delivered for the purpose of venting anger and exerting power. Spanking is *about the child*—delivered for the purpose of encouraging a submissive heart.

Q: Are there children for whom spanking is not a good idea?
A: Yes. The behavior of neurologically impaired children (e.g., those with attention-deficit/hyperactivity disorder [ADHD]) may actually worsen because of a spanking. Children who have been abused and those extremely sensitive also need a different approach.[4]

Q: Are there legal ramifications if I spank my child?
A: It all depends on the country or state in which you live. Corporal punishment has been banned or restricted in many countries,[5] and in 2012, Delaware became the first state to define child abuse as any act that causes a child "pain," effectively outlawing parental spanking.[6] However, laws change—they can be enacted, challenged, overturned, and reenacted. Be aware of current legislation in your area.

Remember this encouragement from God's Word: "And have you forgotten the encouraging words God spoke to you as his children? He said, 'My child, don't make light of the LORD's discipline, and don't give up when he corrects you'" (Heb. 12:5 NLT).

Making a List and Checking It Twice

As you stock your toolkit for implementing firm and fair boundaries, consider creating a *written list* of rewards and repercussions, knowing the list will change as your children mature.

Rewards. Many parents invite their children's involvement in selecting their rewards from a list of possibilities. Include affordable, realistic rewards, prioritized into three groups: major rewards, everyday rewards, and tiny rewards.[7] Matching the reward to the positive behavior will help children gain a more concrete grasp of the cause and effects of their choices.

Experiment to find out what means the most to each child. For one child, it could be one-on-one time with you. To another, it could be writing affirming words or a poem for your child. To still another, a small gift. Years ago, I devised "the 5 Ts" to speak another person's *language of love*: time, talk, touch, tokens, and tasks. Discern the primary *T* language for each family member. Then use rewards within these five categories—and be creative!

Repercussions. Don't allow kids to pick their own repercussions. Effective consequences require adult discretion. (In addition, human nature will prompt children to select the least painful repercussion, not necessarily the most effective!) I do believe, however, that having a list, sorted into categories that make sense for your family, can be very helpful.

•   •   •

Since no two children are exactly alike, effective boundaries, rewards, and repercussions for each child will differ. Consider the age of your child. Was this a first "offense" or the fifth? Is repentance or defiance present? These are just a few of the questions you'll want to contemplate when selecting rewards and repercussions. Like a prospector panning for gold, I invite you to discover the "nuggets"—those golden ideas that bring out the best in *your* child.

Checkpoint

What has shaped your attitudes about rewards and repercussions? Your childhood experiences? The Bible? Other factors? Whatever the answer, take heart! As you seek to instruct and teach your children, your heavenly Father promises, "I will instruct you and teach you in the way you should go; I will counsel you with my loving eye on you" (Ps. 32:8 NIV).

Questions and Answers about Boundaries

Questions about boundaries are common among parents. If you settle these questions now, you need not suffer from self-doubt later—especially when you need confidence to stand your ground. When I was a youth director, parents most often asked me the following boundary-related questions.

Q: Will Boundaries Limit My Child's Creativity?

A: No. In fact, exactly the opposite is true. Kids are like kites.[1] They struggle to become independent and "airborne," yet, all the while, they must have the stability from the string (boundaries) or they will crash! *God designed your role as a parent to prepare your kite for flight.*[2]

As evidence of this principle, I'm reminded of a pastor who allowed his artistic son free reign without boundaries. The boy could draw on the walls, doors—anything. Now in his midtwenties, the young man has tattooed his entire face, to the point that he cannot obtain employment except as a tattoo artist.

Creativity flourishes within the safety of encouragement, unconditional love, and appropriate boundaries. In reality, no one outgrows the need for love and limits—boundaries express both. The apostle Paul recognized the need for encouraging those closest to him—those under his care: "Like a father with his children, we exhorted each one of you and encouraged you and charged you to walk in a manner worthy of God, who calls you into his own kingdom and glory" (1 Thess. 2:11–12).

Q: Won't Boundaries Increase Stress on Everyone?

A: No.[3] "When a youngster discovers there is no threat behind the millions of words he hears, he stops listening. . . . The only messages he responds to are those reaching a peak of emotion, which means there is much screaming and yelling going on."[4]

Boundaries eliminate the need for parents to argue, fight, and scream—self-defeating behaviors that are both counterproductive and emotionally depleting.

Instead of making up rules as you go, operating with fair and firm boundaries makes a significant portion of parenting *automatic*. Once you set the boundaries, kids know what's expected of them, as well as the related rewards and repercussions. As a result, *they* choose whether to obey or not. Therefore *they* (not you) *choose* whether they will receive the reward or repercussion.

Q: How Soon after Kids Cross a Boundary Should They Receive the Repercussion?

A: As soon as possible. Acting immediately helps your kids connect the wrong behavior with the right repercussion.

Q: How Can I First Lay the Foundation for Boundaries to Work?[5]

A: To lay the foundation for boundaries:

Verbalize unconditional love. Assure your children that even though you won't always like what they do, you will always love and value them. Daily communicate this unconditional love, even if your children don't respond or reciprocate (John 13:34).

Show respect. Respect is a two-way street. If you want them to have respect for you, show respect to them. Accept their need for—and right to have—dignity. Knock on their doors before entering their rooms. When old enough, give them bathroom privacy. Listen attentively to what they say and how they feel (1 Pet. 2:17).

Empower. Making choices helps children gain wisdom. Instill the belief that their wise choices can make a positive difference in the lives of others as well as in their own lives. Based on their choices to honor the boundaries, give them more freedom to make more and more choices (Deut. 30:19).

Invest time. Spend time collectively and separately with your children to establish a foundation for boundaries. Enjoy and get to know them better. Plan meaningful outings and activities. Ask them to share their views and get to know and be a part of their world (1 Thess. 2:8).

Listen. Children long to be heard but often don't have words to express their thoughts and feelings. Listening can help you identify what is going on. Insecurity, fearfulness, depression, and many misbehaviors are motivated by deep, unspoken needs. Be attentive and compassionate, listening with your heart and asking yourself, *What are my children really saying?* Check for shared understanding by mirroring back to your child what you heard them say. "What I heard is _____. Is that what you meant?" (Prov. 1:5).

Problem solve. Be patient. Realize your children's behavior reflects their emotional, physical, and spiritual development. Their brains respond emotionally rather than rationally. Disruptive actions are their misguided attempts to solve a perceived problem. Help them learn to identify their *true* problems and find acceptable ways to solve them.

Evaluate the reasons your children give for violating boundaries, refusing to excuse or to accept weak justification for willful wrongdoing (see "What Is the Difference between Helping and

Rescuing?" on p. 33). Modify boundaries that are ineffective (Job 34:4).

Pray. Pray that the boundaries you establish for your children will be fair, effective, and firm—based on God's truth—and that your own beliefs and behaviors do not violate a boundary set by God. Pray that your convictions and communication with your kids reflect the character of Christ (Col. 4:2).

Q: What Steps Are Involved in Setting Boundaries?

A: It's essential that you and your children share the same understanding about what you expect in your home. These four steps will enable you to implement fair and effective boundaries.[6]

Clarify expectations—what is everyone's role?

1. Talk with your children about what they can expect from you: You will prioritize them, providing food, shelter, clothing as well as love, encouragement, and limits (boundaries).
2. Explain what you expect of them.
3. Write down the agreed-upon expectations.
4. Have everyone sign the agreement acknowledging that each person understands and commits to honor the established boundaries (Isa. 33:6). (See House Rules on p. 31 for an example.)

Q: Is There Such a Thing As a Bad Boundary?

A: Yes.[7] To be effective, boundaries must be reasonable and age-appropriate. *An unreasonable boundary* would be a parent who insists that a child be in bed by nine o'clock on Friday night when the ball game they're attending at school isn't even over until nine o'clock. That's too restrictive. Likewise, parents who don't enforce a reasonable bedtime on school nights are being too lenient. They aren't doing what's best for their child.

Make the "punishment fit the crime" and be responsive to your child's unique temperament. For example, seeing a stern expression on your face will lead some children to instant repentance, while others might learn better by a time-out from their activities. Repercussions and rewards aren't one-size-fits-all.

Certain boundaries will need to change as your child matures. As you prayerfully seek godly wisdom and observe your child, you will be able to discern God's will for specific situations. However, once you adopt an appropriate boundary, repercussions and rewards must be clearly communicated and carried out—*without apology.*

Q: How Can I Explain to My Child the Need for Boundaries?

A: Over the years, I've shared a story with people of *all* ages—with great results.[8] "Imagine a clever young goldfish gurgling, 'I want to be free of this *fishbowl!*' I don't like the boundary of this bowl! It's keeping me from going where I want to go and doing what I want to do—it's too limiting!'

"So, one day the goldfish jumps a little here and leaps a little there. Finally, with the flip of his fins and a flap of his tail, he leaps outside the bowl.

"Now the fish is free! He's cleared the boundary of the fishbowl.

"But now what happens to our little goldfish? Within minutes he dies. This one single act doomed him to certain death. Why?

1. Goldfish need water.
2. The fishbowl held the needed water.
3. The boundary of the fishbowl held the water the goldfish needed for life."

I conclude the story by saying, "Being free to do whatever you want may *seem* right, but that doesn't make it right. As Proverbs 14:12 says, 'There is a way that appears to be right, but in the end it leads to death' (NIV). God gave you to me and me to you. Part of my job is helping you *stay in the bowl* God has given you. As you grow, God has designed your bowl to grow right along with you so it will always be just the right size!"

Checkpoint

Even though we have our children with us longer than any other species on the planet, all too soon babies are grown. We may have only eighteen birthdays with them living in our home. Eighteen Christmases. Eighteen summers. What boundaries do you need to initiate today to enhance the priceless moments you have with your children? Jesus said, "What father among you, if his son asks for a fish, will instead of a fish give him a serpent?" (Luke 11:11). A good father will indeed give his son a fish; a great father will take the time to teach his son to fish. Realize, Jesus said, "Follow me and *I will make you fishers of men*" (Matt. 4:19).

Section 2

Building Beneficial Boundaries

"For the moment all discipline seems
painful rather than pleasant,
but later it yields the peaceful fruit
of righteousness to those
who have been trained by it."

(Heb. 12:11)

6

Anger and Aggression

When your preschooler, Brady, thrust out his arms and jumped off the couch yelling, "Supah Heewoe!" you laughed at his adorable superhero imitation. But then he began karate chopping and kicking his classmates, making him anything but adorable to them—not to mention the teachers and parents.

In fact, aggression has become Brady's immediate response to almost everything and everyone. Just today you received a call from his teacher stating that Brady pushed his classmate off the playground slide, spraining her wrist. And he is also getting a reputation for picking fights. If this provoking behavior continues, Brady will find himself suspended or possibly even expelled from preschool.

What Are Contributing Factors?

Numerous elements can contribute to childhood anger, aggression, and fighting. Here are common culprits:

- Feelings of hurt, injustice, fear, or frustration are the root causes of anger, which is actually a secondary emotion.[1]
- A child might express *outside* the home any anger, aggression, and/or fighting that is occurring *inside* the home, and vice versa.
- Children may default to aggression if they've not been taught acceptable and constructive ways to handle emotions, how to make friends, and how to interact socially.

- Many children hit, kick, or even bite during the process of exploring the world around them as a means of testing various behaviors to see which ones are acceptable and effective in getting what they want.
- Children who feel inferior, inadequate, or constricted in some way may act out their frustration through aggressive behavior. So may a child with a hearing impairment, ADHD, learning disability, or other difficulty.
- Aggression inhibits the ability to empathize with another's pain resulting in failure to develop connected relationships. Such a child continuously feels isolated, then reacts with aggression . . . perpetuating the cycle.

Ask yourself: *Where and when does my child's anger, aggression, and/or fighting emerge?* Does the behavior occur only at school or is it also happening at home? If the problem is predominantly at home, examine the family dynamics:

- How do you and your child relate to one another?
- How do you and your spouse relate?
- How do you express anger toward your child and others?
- What is the interaction like between siblings?
- Is your child aggressive toward everyone or just one person?
- Is he exploiting the position as oldest sibling or defending against being bullied as the youngest?
- Is the behavior consistent or does it show up only occasionally, during times of stress?

A child with a physical or neurological disorder typically demonstrates aggression both inside and outside the home. If you suspect a problem may exist, talk to your child's pediatrician.

Once you determine *where* the aggressive behavior occurs, ask: Is the behavior merely a bad habit that needs breaking, or is there genuine anger behind it? Is my child hurting others because *he* is hurting in some area—physically, emotionally, or psychologically? After all, it's often said that "hurt people *hurt* people."

What Could You Do?

Unchecked anger and aggression generally lead to more aggression, fighting, and alienation, underscoring the importance of helping your child learn to manage his emotions and behavior *while he's still young*. To do this, consider these suggestions:

- Don't ignore hurtful, inappropriate aggression in male children by thinking *boys will be boys*.
- Get your child's side of the story. Ask him to tell you about any incidents of aggression or fighting.
- Discuss with your child's teachers how you can work together to redirect your child's behavior. Bring your child into this meeting. Encourage him to share his thoughts on how he can be more respectful of others. Recap the boundaries and the associated rewards and repercussions.
- Talk to the parents of the children who have experienced your child's aggression. Apologize and assure them you're working to prevent further episodes. Take your child to apologize to the children he's intimidated or hurt, including their parents. Have him take "peace offering" gifts for each of the children—something he has made or purchased himself.
- If he has used words to hurt, he is to think of a way to use words to heal. Perhaps he can write a note, make a card, sing a song, or share a story.
- If he has used his hands or feet to hurt, ask to find ways to use his hands or feet to help whomever he hurt (carry an item, help tidy up, bring a snack, etc.).
- Provide age-appropriate ways for your child to release his energy and exercise his body, such as sports, gymnastics, running, or swimming. This will help you determine whether the behavior stems from pent-up energy, emotional pain, or other factors.
- If anger, aggression, or fighting occur only when your child is with a specific child, alert the other child's parents to see if you can work together to build a healthy friendship. If not, you may need to help your child find a new friend.

- Teach and model good problem-solving and anger-resolution skills—with your child and with all other members of your family. Explain that aggression and fighting are never options for settling differences. When you're upset, continue to be respectful.
- Help your child explore what he was feeling. Many children (adults too) will struggle to name their feelings. A chart that encourages your child to pick a face showing what he's feeling can help. Find sample charts online by searching for "children's play therapy feelings chart."
- Don't discipline in anger.
- Be fair, but also very clear that there are strong repercussions for inappropriate behavior, depending on the nature and severity of the incident.
- Sincerely affirm your child's strides toward peaceful resolutions.
- Encourage your child to "put on" the full armor of God outlined in Ephesians 6:10–18, empowering him to stand strong for the cause of good and righteousness. To help him visualize the armor, draw, make, or purchase an armor costume.[2] Together, memorize the Ephesians passage and others that promote godly conflict resolution.
- Watch an upbeat superhero movie together. Point out that superheroes use their super strength and abilities to protect and help, never to harm another, except when necessary for a greater good. Contrast the movie's superhero with the antagonist. Ask how the "bad guy" acts toward others. What is the end result of being cruel?
- Include your child in household chores. Invite him to help you find a neighbor or relative who needs household tasks done and who would welcome your child's "heroic" energy and enthusiasm. He'll feel a sense of satisfaction from using his energy productively.
  - Give loving encouragement anytime you see your "superhero" use his power for good.
- A child's whole world can become chaotic if his parents aren't getting along. When you and your mate disagree, let your child observe you working to reach a speedy, peaceful resolution that honors both parties.[3]

– Of course, some conflicts can't be resolved quickly. In such cases, respectfully agree to continue the conversation later, making sure your child hears you say how important it is to work things out. Once your conflict *has* been resolved, let your child know that "Mommy and Daddy listened to each other and found a way to work through our disagreement. Everything is okay."

• Should the aggression continue or escalate, seek professional help to screen for underlying factors (e.g., oppositional defiant disorder—persistent arguing and angry or disruptive behavior toward authority figures[4]).

What Could You Say?

Even if you determine that your child's aggression is a reaction to an area of hurt in his own life, it's *never* an acceptable excuse for hurting others. As you discuss the angry episode with your child, you could say, "Son, I'm sorry you're hurting. But that's *not* a reason to hurt someone else. Feeling angry isn't wrong. We all feel that way sometimes. God made anger to work like a warning light in your heart. It tells us something needs attention.

"If your toy's low-battery light comes on, what would happen if you didn't pay attention to it?" [Wait for your child to tell you the toy would stop working.] "Exactly! The light tells us there's a problem, so we can fix it. That's how anger works. It tells us there's a problem in our lives that needs fixing.

"The Bible says, 'Be angry, and do not sin' (Ps. 4:4). When you feel angry, or feel like hurting someone, you can talk to God and to me to help you find ways to fix what's causing the anger. I'll listen to anything you have to say—even if you think that I'm part of the problem. But you may not take out your anger on others or on me.

"Let's talk about better ways to deal with this. What are some of your own ideas?" [Listen and discuss.] "Let's pray and ask God for his help. I'm here to help too. I love you and I know you can choose to be kind."

In the case of your son, who pushed his friend and fought on the playground, you could say, "It's fun to pretend you're a superhero. Did you know the most important thing a superhero does is help and protect people?

"Remember how you felt when [name a painful incident] happened?" [Allow him to answer.] "You don't like to be hurt. No one does. It's wrong to hurt others. You're not to hit or kick any living thing—animals or people.

"Because you chose to hurt [name of his classmate] today, you won't have playtime tonight. You'll use the time to think about two kind things you can do for [name] to begin making up for hurting her.

"After dinner, we're going to [name's] house to check on her and for you to apologize and ask her to forgive you. Then you'll offer to do any chores she can't do because of her hurt wrist.

"I love you and I'm sure you can learn to use your strength to help people, just like real superheroes do. I'll be praying for you. In fact, let's pray together right now!"

Wisdom from God's Word

Children view aggression on television programs, movies, video games, and the news. Like mirrors, they reflect what they see. To counter this attitude, spend time reading through the Beatitudes in Matthew 5:1–12 with your child. Fill your child's heart with the values Christ spoke and lived so that as your child grows, these will be reflected in his life. "Let the peace of Christ rule in your hearts, to which indeed you were called in one body. And be thankful" (Col. 3:15).

See these related chapters:
Chapter 4: "Your R & R Toolkit," page 38
Chapter 9: "Biting," page 76
Chapter 10: "Bullying," page 79

7

Back Talk

Several friends with their children meet at your home for a fun-filled outing. The picnic basket is placed in the car, and you call the kids to get ready to leave. Electronic game in hand, your seven-year-old daughter heads—barefoot—out the door.

"Shandra, get your shoes."

"You get 'em," she calls back, planting a hand on her hip, "and bring my headband too."

Hearing those words and watching her defiant body language sends your temperature soaring. Your daughter is talking back . . . again. It's disheartening, demeaning, and totally disrespectful. But how do you make it stop?

What Could You Do?

Accept that you are responsible for taking the initiative to stop your child's unacceptable behavior. As a parent, *you* decide how your child will treat you. Don't assume a teacher or a coach will curb your child's sassy predisposition. Your daughter chooses to speak respectfully to certain grown-ups—a neighbor, grandparent, or instructor—but chooses to speak disrespectfully to you because you have not yet given her a reason to do otherwise. Your child talks back to you . . . because she *can*.

Nor will she outgrow talking back to you. In fact, if left unchecked, the problem will become worse in her teens and continue into adulthood. So you must set clear and consistent boundaries *now* before this behavior escalates. Here's how:

• Curb back talk at the first retort. Many parents fear their child will not like them if they prohibit back talk. Others don't want to make their child "feel bad." In reality, your child will be happier and respect you *more* when boundaries are set and steadfastly enforced.

• Do not respond with smart-aleck comments of your own. Instead model wisdom and maturity with your choice of words.

• If your child sasses you more than she does your spouse, examine the rewards and repercussions your spouse uses and consider implementing them yourself.

   – If you are the stronger parent, back your spouse by reinforcing the requirement for respectful behavior.

• Occasionally, your child will have strong negative feelings about a decision you've made. This is to be expected. Teach her how to express these feelings, along with all others, *respectfully*, without the use of back talk. (You have an opportunity to model this every time *you're* angry.)

• Make the repercussion as immediate as possible. For instance, if you're at an event, disengage the child from the activities for a time. If you're at a restaurant, take your child away from the table until she can agree to speak respectfully. When your child is with friends, have her sit out of the playtime activity for a specified time. Leave the store if back talk is a problem while shopping. In each situation, explain that an apology to you is needed and that disrespectful words and behavior will not be tolerated.

   – Help your child understand that back talk is never acceptable in *any* situation. Confront any back talk that occurs in public just as straightforwardly as if you were in private. Otherwise, your child will quickly learn she can sass you in front of others because you will permit it.

   – If back talk continues after you've made your position clear on a particular issue, begin suspending your child's privileges and canceling planned activities.

– Be consistent and fair. Don't accept back talk one day
and overreact to it the next. Once your child experiences
your firm boundaries and understands that outbursts
won't be tolerated, the frequency will lessen.

In response to your daughter's back talk, described in the opening scenario, you could also leave her at home if an adult will be
there to care for her while you go to the park.

What Could You Say?

Assuming your daughter is accompanying you to the park, you
could say, "I know you can speak respectfully. I was proud when
you [describe a recent time when she responded without back talk].
That's very different from the way you spoke to me a moment ago.
What did I ask you to do?" [Wait for a candid reply.] "That's right.
I told you to get your shoes. But instead of obeying, what did you
say?" After your daughter tells you, say, "That response was sassy
and disrespectful.

"When we arrive at the park, you'll sit instead of play. It's clear
you need time to think about how you chose to speak to me. If
you want to play with your friends and your video game, you'll
first need to tell me how you could have spoken respectfully. What
words could you have used? And you'll need to apologize for your
back talk.

"Now please go find your shoes and take them to the car. And
give me your video game.

"I love you and I want you to be able to enjoy yourself at the
park. When you show me you can speak to me with respect, I'll
know you are ready for this privilege."

Wisdom from God's Word

Scripture describes the good—and the harm—our words can do.
"With the tongue we praise our Lord and Father, and with it
we curse human beings, who have been made in God's likeness"

(James 3:9 NIV). Loving parents help their children discipline their tongue at an early age. "Don't use foul or abusive language. Let everything you say be good and helpful, so that your words will be an encouragement to those who hear them" (Eph. 4:29 NLT).

See these related chapters:
Chapter 6: "Anger and Aggression," page 61
Chapter 17: "Disrespectfulness," page 117

8

Bedtime Battles

At bedtime, five-year-old Bart dawdles and dallies. Then, as you are busy helping the baby into pajamas, big brother squirts toothpaste into the fishbowl and stirs enthusiastically with his Batman toothbrush.

The family fish, Nemo, is not happy . . . and neither are you! Where is the *bedtime nanny* when you need her?

What Could You Do?

When it comes to bedtime, in general, you need to know that the three Rs are *routine, routine,* and *routine.* Find a short, simple routine that works for your family and *stick with it.* Research shows that children who go to bed late or at irregular times are more likely to have behavioral problems—all because of inconsistent bedtimes . . . in much the same way that adults experience jet lag.[1]

If your child's bedroom has become a war zone at bedtime and you are weary from battle fatigue, here are age-appropriate steps to restore peace.

Five-Year-Olds and Younger
- Help your child unwind for bed before he gets his "second wind." If initial bedtime sleepiness passes without your child making it into bed, he can get a fresh burst of energy.

- Research shows that a hormone called melatonin, which causes drowsiness, begins to increase in young children between 7 p.m. and 8 p.m. Light emitted by television and computers can suppress melatonin. Be sure to turn the technology off well before bedtime.[2]
- Give your child fair warning that playtime is coming to a close. "Five more minutes and then we'll get ready for bed."
- Sing a song together as you put away toys to help your child shift from playtime to bedtime.
- Lay out clothes for the next day. If your child shows an interest in clothing, limit options to a manageable number and let him choose. Ask, "Tomorrow, do you want to wear your red shirt or the yellow one?" Then, honor his choice.
- Water is a natural tranquilizer. Include a bath or shower in your child's bedtime routine.
- If your child is distracted, play a subdued version of peek-a-boo as you pull pajamas over his head.
- Brush and floss. Sing a song to your child while he's brushing. When the familiar song ends, he will know it's time to stop brushing. Count teeth while flossing.
- Let your child pick a specific number of books you can read to him. For example, a three-year-old can choose three short books, while a four-year-old might select four books.
- When your child gets ready for bed on time (or even beats the clock), the reward can be extra reading time.
  - Because of the vital importance of reading, don't routinely cut back on bedtime reading as a repercussion.
  - Instead, subtract playtime before bed and remove distractions until your child routinely gets to bed on time.
- Try tucking your child into bed by creating a make-believe ice cream sundae: Getting into bed is the ice cream. The top sheet is the hot fudge, the blanket is the whipped cream, and the comforter is the cherry on top.
- Regardless of a child's behavior, showing affection, saying "I love you," and having prayer time are essential. Your child needs to know that your love is unconditional.

- Pray aloud for your child. Let him hear how thankful you are for the gift he is in your life and mention a positive character trait.
- Encourage your child to pray and thank God for specific things. Ask God for help with problems.
- If your child has separation issues when you leave the bedroom, give him some choices. "Would you like your nightlight on or off?" "Do you want your door open or closed?"

Older Children

- Provide a list of steps for your child to follow at bedtime and empower him to make choices. For instance, say, "I'm putting you in charge of getting yourself ready for bed. You can choose to do these steps in whatever order you like as long as you are finished by bedtime."
- For a perfectionist or procrastinator, place an analog clock in the bathroom. Show him how much time he has for each step of the process. (Children don't have an internal sense of time, and timers can induce stress, so analog clocks are best for helping children associate time with particular tasks.)
- If your child is angry about something that occurred during the day, encourage him to forgive his offender(s) and release his anger to God, asking for his help with the issue. Tell him you're available to talk about it if he'd like.
- Once tucked in bed, allow older children to enjoy books, reading chapters aloud over several evenings.
- Tell your child endearing stories about when he was younger. Share memories about your own childhood and stories about other family members.
- Make up tales together. On occasion, you can start the story, your child can add to it and then toss the story back to you as the two of you "build a tale" together.
- If your child enjoys reading, allow him to read by himself for an additional half hour before turning out the light. (Back up bedtime to accommodate the extra reading time.)
- Some children enjoy listening to audio books as they go to sleep.

In the case of your son, who stirred the fish bowl at bedtime, address both the *misbehavior* and the *motivation* behind it.

- Remove the fishbowl from his room.
- Was this an openly defiant act of disobedience intended to cause harm? If so, swift repercussion is in order.
- Whether out of defiance or a sudden burst of energy (a second wind), have your son help you clean the fish bowl.

What Could You Say?

"I want you to be able to enjoy pets like Nemo, but having pets means treating them well. Why was stirring the fishbowl with your toothbrush wrong?" [Listen and respond appropriately.]

"I'm disappointed that you chose to mistreat Nemo. God made fish to eat fish food, not toothpaste. And he made children to drink pure water, not fish water. What you did could have hurt Nemo and you. I want you to choose never to do that again. Will you?" [Wait for the reply.]

"I've put Nemo in another bowl with fresh water. Tomorrow you'll help clean the fishbowl so we can put him back in his home. Having a pet fish is a privilege. Once you show me you can take good care of Nemo, we can put him back in your room and maybe think about buying more fish.

"Because you chose to disrupt bedtime, starting tomorrow night, you'll have less time to play. That way, you can start getting ready for bed fifteen minutes earlier. And if that's still not enough time, we'll make it thirty minutes. When you choose to get ready for bed on time, your reward will be getting to play longer before bedtime.

"Play more before bed or less or none at all. It's up to you. Let's pray tonight for God to help you with this. I know He will . . . and so will I.

"Let's thank the Lord for what the Bible says, 'In peace I will both lie down and sleep; for you alone O LORD, make me dwell in safety.'"

Wisdom from God's Word

Bedtime should be a sweet ending to the day, a time when hearts draw close, hurts are released, and offenses forgiven. With a few simple steps, you can create a peaceful setting that enables your child to sleep securely. Many parents have observed that their children sleep better when Scripture is included as part of the bedtime routine and when the day is closed with prayer. Start these practices when your child is young in order to nurture a lifelong heart for God. "If you lie down, you will not be afraid; when you lie down, your sleep will be sweet" (Prov. 3:24).

9

Biting

Your sister-in-law and her young son have come to visit from out of state. Thrilled for your three-year-old daughter, Amy, to get to know her same-aged cousin, you're also excited for your sister-in-law to see, firsthand, how loving and kind your little girl is. While the cousins explore the toy box, you grab the camera. These pictures will be perfect for the family Christmas card!

But as the camera focuses on the darling duo, you can't believe the scene you're seeing through the viewfinder. Rather than kissing cousin Charlie on the cheek, Amy bites him—*hard*! As your nephew howls in pain, your sister-in-law rushes in to the rescue.

Stunned, you try to understand . . . what in the world just happened? What got into your "sweet" little girl? And how do you prevent a repeat performance?

What Could You Do?

Typically, biting is a temporary behavior in children until around age three. Reasons for biting vary from teething and hurting gums to frustration at not having the words to express themselves to simple curiosity and experimentation. All of these behaviors are normal. Biting does not mean your child has serious social or psychological problems or that you should feel like a failure about your own parenting skills. So what do you do?

If your child is known to bite:

- Closely supervise her when she is with other children.
- When you see your little biter ready to nip, quickly intervene by saying firmly, "No biting."
- Watch for any signals that your child is about to bite. For example, some children clench their teeth immediately beforehand.
- Once you have your child's attention, help her find something constructive to do by offering a distraction, such as a toy.
- If she bites or attempts to bite again, repeat, "No! No biting." If possible, immediately take your child home or remove her from the other children to help her associate biting with the repercussion: No playing with other children—temporarily.
- If your child is teething, give her a refrigerated teething toy or a frozen washcloth to gnaw on.
- If your child exhibits frustration at not being able to express herself appropriately, don't shout back or overreact. Instead, comfort and encourage her. This is a good time to hold your child close and calmly say, "Take your time. Use your words." Then wait patiently and reassure her as she tries.
- Don't give in to tantrums. If you do, your child will *act out* rather than *work out* the problem of using words. Be patient during this phase, calmly but firmly reminding her to "use your words."
- Warning: As a deterrent, a well-intentioned parent of a biting toddler might choose to bite her toddler back. While this unconventional approach would cause a shock effect, it could also reinforce bad behavior—*more biting*. After all, *with children, more is caught than taught.*

What Could You Say?

Since frustration over a lack of language skills often underlies biting—especially as children begin trying to talk—use spoken language to guide your child to the correct behavior.

"Honey, no! No biting. Play nicely. Use your words to tell me what you want."

When your child reaches to take another child's toy and appears ready to bite, say, "No! No biting! We use our mouths to talk nicely to people, not to bite people. Biting is for chewing food. We use our hands to hold the ball. When Charlie is playing with a toy, you may find another toy to play with. Look, here's a ball! Let's play with this ball."

Wisdom from God's Word

When is the last time you saw a grown-up biting another person? (Never!) Exactly! Take heart—this too shall pass. The Bible says, "For everything there is a season, and a time for every matter under heaven" (Eccles. 3:1). Yes, this biting season will pass.

So to turn the tide on your young biter, use these wise words: "Jesus said, 'Love one another'" (John 13:34). Since love means doing what's best for others, let's do what's best—and not bite! Then every day, say it together, "Love one another!"

See Chapter 40: "Temper Tantrums," page 234

10

Bullying

Sitting in the principal's office, you're told that your son, Ben, is picking on a shy boy with a speech impediment, and he's half Ben's size.[1] Ben called the boy humiliating names, forced him to smell Ben's gym socks, and made fun of the student's stuttering.

Now the teacher and principal are waiting for you to tell them what you're going to do about the situation. How can you provide boundaries that will make a difference when your child is away from home and at school all day?

How Much Do You Tolerate?

The answer is *none*. Set a zero-tolerance for bullying by holding your child accountable for *all* offensive behavior, any deliberately "hostile physical or verbal activity intended to harm, induce fear, and create terror."[2]

Not surprisingly, bullies typically exploit those they perceive to be physically or psychologically weaker. Inflicting pain or exerting power provides the aggressor with an inflated sense of superiority. Consequently, those who are bullied live with continual fear and expectation of future harassment—or they themselves become bullies to mask their emotional pain.[3] As a parent, it's essential to establish a nonnegotiable boundary forbidding bullying. Whether physical, emotional, or verbal, bullying intimidates, humiliates, and inflicts pain on others.

Regrettably, bullying among children has become epidemic. Seventy-four percent of eight- to eleven-year-old students report that bullying occurs at their schools.[4]

Be acutely aware that types of bullying differ at different ages and often with different genders. A young child is more likely to experience physical threats while upper-elementary students have a greater chance of being attacked online, via text, at recess, or during extracurricular events. Bullying can consist of:

- Physical attacks: Pushing, striking, injuring, damaging property and possessions.
- Verbal attacks: Using cruel words or a harsh tone to insult and inflict emotional pain.
- Emotional attacks: Shunning, ostracizing, ignoring, using demeaning gestures, and using dominating or dismissive behavior.
- Cyber attacks: Posting, texting, e-mailing, and sending damaging messages or photos via social networks.

Look for signs that your child is bullying others:

- Be aware of your child's attitudes and actions.
- Listen to conversations he has with friends or even acquaintances.
- Check e-mails, text messages, and website activity (see chap. 26, "Media Mania" on p. 164).
- Note any recurring doodling or drawings that seem dark or mean-spirited.
- Notice if your child's choice of clothing styles or colors changes to fit in with an undesirable group.
- Look for marks on your child's body, such as drawing tattoos, piercings, and burns that could signify affiliation with a group of bullies or a gang.

What Could You Do?

Some childhood problems are best left to children to solve. But bullying is *not* one of them! If your child's school does not yet have a program addressing bullying, organize parents to partner with the school and start one.

In addition, you could:

- Encourage your child's school authorities to ensure adults are present when vulnerable children are at risk. *Do not* leave self-restraint completely up to the conscience or ability of kids to "work it out."[5]
- Talk to your child, clearly stating your expectations, along with firm, fair boundaries.
- Try to determine how and where your child *learned* to bully (since bullying is a learned behavior). Was it at after-school care, at home, elsewhere? If you believe the answer may be "at home," begin working immediately to rid your home environment of bullying. You can tell a child not to bully, but if he sees the behavior at home, your words will be ineffective.
- Help your child discover the motivation behind his bullying. What's the emotional pay-off for him? What unmet need is he trying to meet? Is it personal, social (perhaps peer pressure is a factor), or something else?
- Watch for patterns of gossip, meanness, cliquish behavior, and aggression. If these surface, help your child break harmful habits through long-term mentoring that includes teaching biblical patterns for communication.
- Through role play, encourage your child to use words skillfully to resolve conflict. Help him practice saying things kindly.
- Help your child empathize with his victim(s). Although he knows he is hurting the other person, he may not understand how deeply.
  - If he's kindergarten age or younger, it's likely your child's not mature enough to grasp the long-term effects of his actions. Help him think about how he would feel if *he* were being bullied. Appeal to his conscience and explain the deep pain he's causing.
- Involve your child in constructive groups and community service activities—scouting, sports, band, church youth groups—whatever best suits his talents and interests. Serve as a volunteer

in these activities to build common connections and to observe how your child interacts with others.

- Remember: Repercussions without a solid relationship foster additional anger, rebellion, and resentment. Nurture your relationship with your child. Spend quality time with him. Read aloud, include him on errands, play board games, require yard work, do household chores, family activities, and visits with family and friends. His unacceptable behavior proves that he needs more governance and parental guidance.

- Share Scripture to help redirect your child's angry, aggressive thoughts. With your child, memorize Romans 12:2 using a translation easy for him to understand: ".Don't copy the behavior and customs of this world, but let God transform you into a new person by changing the way you think. Then you will learn to know God's will for you, which is good and pleasing and perfect" (Rom. 12:2 NLT).

- Ask God to soften your child's heart, giving him genuine empathy and concern for others.

- Reward desired attitudes and actions with praise, appreciation, and gradually restored freedom and privileges. Proverbs 9:12 says, "If you become wise, you will be the one to benefit. If you scorn wisdom, you will be the one to suffer" (NLT).

For your son who, as described in the opening scenario, bullied a child at school, you could also:

- Enforce repercussions that are specific, swift, and relevant to the offense.
  - Since your child caused harm, he should offer restitution. This could mean paying double for any damage and performing two kind acts for each offense.
  - Restrict his use of media (television, phone, video games, social networking, etc.) until restitution is complete.

- Take your child to meet with the injured or offended child and his parents. Before the meeting, tell your child he must take responsibility for his actions and apologize.

What Could You Say?

In the case of your son caught bullying a classmate, you could say, "I'm always proud when you treat others kindly. And I've seen you do it!" [Share a recent example.]

"Your teacher told me about how you treated [name of the bullied child] today. I'd like to hear your thoughts about what happened." [Listen for clues to help eliminate the bullying at its root.]

"What you did today is bullying. Bullying hurts other people . . . and it hurts you, too. The Bible says to 'treat others as you would want them to treat you' (Matt. 7:12 NET). How did you feel when [describe a time when someone was mean to your child]? When you hurt others, it makes me sad and it makes God sad too."

Next, lead your child to the kitchen. Pour some sugar on top of a hard, dry sponge. Then ask:

"What happened when I poured sugar on this sponge?"

[Your child will observe that the sugar bounced off immediately.]

"Exactly! The sugar wasn't able to soak into the sponge."

[Now, wet the sponge and pour sugar on it.]

"What happens to the sugar this time when I pour it on the sponge?"

[Your child will observe that the sugar soaks in.]

"This sponge is like your heart. At first, when you choose to hurt others, you'll know it's wrong. That's God speaking to you! If you pay attention and stop, your heart will be soft and you'll have the joy of closeness with God. But if you keep choosing to do what you know is wrong, your heart will get hard and dry like this sponge. You won't be able to soak in the joy of God in your life. Instead, you'll feel numb, sad, and angry. What do you want to choose for your heart—softness and joy . . . or hardness and sadness?

"Actions have consequences. Because you chose to bully, you'll do two acts of kindness for the boy you hurt in order to try to make it up to him. That is called *restitution*. You'll also apologize and replace anything you damaged, paying for it with your own money.

If you don't have the money, you'll earn it by doing jobs around the house.

"Bullying is wrong and it must stop right now. It's against the rules at school, at home, and in the Bible. I love you too much to allow you to keep bullying others. Understand that if you continue to be hurtful, you'll be choosing not to play with your friends and to sit out of playtime at school.

"Let's talk about what you're going to do to solve this problem. What are your ideas?

"When you choose to treat people the way you want to be treated, you'll have a soft heart and good friendships that are blessed by God. I know you can make these changes. Let's pray right now for God to help you."

Wisdom from God's Word

As a parent, your most important job is to cultivate humility and the heart of Christ into the heart of your child. The Bible is blatantly clear about God's opposition to bullies and bullying behavior . . . "Likewise, you who are younger, be subject to the elders. Clothe yourselves, all of you, with humility toward one another, for 'God opposes the proud but gives grace to the humble.' Humble yourselves, therefore, under the mighty hand of God so that at the proper time he might exalt you, casting all your anxieties on him, because he cares for you" (1 Pet. 5:5–6).

See these related chapters:

11

Car Etiquette

You're driving your children to an amusement park where you will drop them off to spend the day with your sister and her kids. Then you will head to a birthday lunch with friends. Suddenly a pint-sized tennis shoe careens from the back seat and lands in your cup of hot coffee—splashing it all over your freshly pressed clothes.

Your voice reverberates throughout the car, demanding a halt to the chaos. Stopping on the side of the road to clean up, your anger boils.

What is it about being cooped up in a car that brings out the worst in children?

What Could You Do?

As with most other areas of discipline, car wars must be won before the battle ever begins. Before you leave the house, it's best to review the boundaries you've established for acceptable behavior in the car.

- Children's ears have an uncanny ability to tune out anything resembling a lecture. So, make remembering the rules fun. For instance, you might teach your children to sing them or make them rhyme, occasionally offering a prize for the child who can recite them. Create an acrostic built around the word CARS:

C is for caring that others have a good ride; *A* is for adjusting my voice; *R* is for remembering what items to bring with me; *S* is for safety, always a good choice!

- Once the car is in motion, focus on driving, not reviewing rules. If you become angry or distracted while driving, you become a danger to yourself, your precious cargo, and others on the road.
- For each child, assemble an activity bag that always stays in the car. Include books, nonmessy snacks, and toys to hold their interest. Individual activity bags will help alleviate fights over who gets what.
- Listen together to inspirational or Christian music.
- Recorded books are wonderful for road trips. While traveling, families can share enjoyable literature and stories.
- Sing songs together.
- Children may want their own headset to listen to music. Grant this request when you are not using the drive time to intentionally connect through singing, conversing, or sharing a recorded book. Ensure their music is age-appropriate and acceptable.
- With the exception of long-distance travel, movies in the car are not recommended. Starting and stopping a movie for short jaunts can result in a lack of concentration and conditions your child not to get involved in the story. This makes it harder to stay attentive while reading and in a classroom setting. Nor is it necessary to continually entertain your child. Perpetual entertainment teaches children to be self-centered, expecting others to be responsible for their emotions and behaviors. (See chap. 26, "Media Mania" on p. 164.)
- If tardiness is an issue, consider waking everyone earlier in order to be able to leave earlier and arrive on time.
- Pulling over for a roadside time-out (where children sit silently to consider required behavior changes) may correct the misbehavior. For toddlers and preschoolers, consider one minute of time-out for every year of the child's age.[1]
  - If the time-out causes your children to arrive late for a fun activity, this may also help them link their actions to the repercussion.

– If misbehavior continues after the time-out—and if your children are *en route* to a fun activity, such as a play date—if possible, turn around and go home.

• "Catch" your children following the rules in the car and praise them to reinforce desirable behavior.

What Could You Say?

In reviewing rules before leaving, ask, "Who can tell me a car rule?" Once a child recites a rule, praise the effort. "Good. That's right! What's another rule?" Acknowledge each child who contributes a rule. Occasionally, sweeten the experience with, "Everyone who remembers the car rules and follows them gets a [name a small reward, see chap. 4, "Your R & R Toolkit" for ideas] when we arrive."

Then say, "Being safe and getting where we're going on time is the biggest reward for following car rules. Remember, if you choose not to follow the rules, you are also choosing to take a time-out . . . or not to go at all."

The first time misbehavior occurs, pull over to a safe place. Resist the urge to lecture with comments such as, "How many times have I told you?" Instead, ask, "What did we say are our car rules?" After reviewing them say, "Which rule did you choose to break?" Listen, then ask, "Do you want to choose to obey the rules now or do you want to choose a time-out?"

If misbehavior occurs again and if going home isn't an option, pull off the road to a safe spot and declare a time-out. Say, "I thought you wanted to enjoy the amusement park today. But if you choose to break the car rules again, there will be no rides with your cousins—only walking around the park with your aunt. I know how much you've been looking forward to this day, and I want you to be able to have a great time. But it's your choice."

Wisdom from God's Word

Rather than the worst of times, traveling in the car can be the best of times. Car rides can deepen family bonds as well as further build positive character traits. Having limited choices while spending time in close proximity to others affords wonderful opportunities to exercise respect and later experience the rewards that accompany it. "Whoever scorns instruction will pay for it but whoever respects a command is rewarded" (Prov. 13:13 NIV).

Cell Phone Struggles

You give your daughter, Stephanie, her first cell phone, but soon afterward you notice troubling changes in her behavior. In the car, she texts when you are talking to her. At her brother's soccer game, she focuses on her phone, not the competition.

When you find her texting in church, you confiscate the phone for a week. And that's when you realize: The Stephanie you once knew is plugged back into the family again. Her sense of humor returns and she spends time with her siblings.

For the first few days after Stephanie gets her phone back—along with clear new usage guidelines—she honors the boundaries. But soon her bad habits return.

One morning, as your daughter sleeps, you pick up her phone and begin browsing through messages. From the photos, texts, and e-mails, you see a consistent thread of deceit and disrespect.

You make up your mind: When Stephanie comes to you in search of her phone, her fixation is going to get . . . *fixed*!

Do Children Need Cell Phones?

As a parent, you may want your child to have a cell phone for a number of reasons, including:

• Protection: enabling your child to reach you in case of an emergency;

- Connection: allowing instant contact at all times;
- Tracking: enabling you to monitor your child's whereabouts through a phone's Global Positioning System (GPS);
- Rite of passage: recognizing that your child has reached a milestone.

What Are the Risks of Giving Your Child a Cell Phone?

It's not uncommon for six-year-olds to know how to send picture messages, communicate with friends, and access information via cell phones.[1] Research shows that for children eight years and older, using a phone to make calls is a secondary interest to texting, listening to music, playing games, sharing photos, and watching videos.[2]

While serving both recreational and practical purposes, cell phones can also transport children to arenas where they do not have the wisdom, maturity, or self-discipline to make informed decisions—places a wise parent would never give them permission to go.

For example, children as young as ten have been known to be involved in "sexting"—sending and receiving text messages with sexually explicit photos. Researchers studying youth sexting concluded: "For young people, the primary technology-related threat is not the 'stranger danger' . . . but technology-mediated sexual pressure from their peers."[3]

Kids today are figuring out how to explore technological frontiers faster than most parents can keep up. In view of the potential risks, children need proactive parental involvement and a clear set of rules to regulate cell phone usage.

Is Your Child Ready for a Cell Phone?

Is your child:

- Mature and responsible at home?
- Doing well in school?
- Likely to exercise discernment (e.g., not disturbing others with personal phone conversations)?
- Likely to obey your rules governing phone usage?

- Unlikely to use a phone to embarrass, harass, or bully others?
- Needing to be in touch with you for safety reasons?

If you answered *yes* to these questions, your child may be ready to use a cell phone responsibly.

What Could You Do?

The following steps can help prepare your child for cell phone safety and success:

- Set a good example with your own cell phone practices. You want your child to be able to do as you *do* not just as you *say*.
- A first phone should be exactly that—a phone and *only* a phone. Save the multiapplication smartphone devices for later. Kid-friendly cell phones make it easier for parents to limit usage, create lists of approved and prohibited numbers, and track a child's location using the phone's GPS.
- For older children who are mature and responsible enough to have phones with added features, set specific guidelines for their use. Also, customize the functions allowed on your child's phone by using parental control features.
- Consider a prepaid cell phone service. This places boundaries on the number of minutes and additional services your child can access.
- Designate with whom your child is allowed to communicate. Initially, limit the contact list to a few trusted people. Over time, enable your child to add contacts but only with your approval.
- Make certain your child knows never to share her personal phone number with anyone without your approval.
- Track your monthly billing statements to monitor your child's usage.
- Make sure your child knows that you will regularly track phone usage footprints. Periodically glance through the phone's contacts, photos, and messages (if the latter two are enabled). Have conversations about how the phone is being used.

- Set age-appropriate boundaries. A younger child should have the phone only when going out and only to communicate with you.
- Consider collecting your child's phone at bedtime and returning it in the morning.
- Discuss which cell phone applications your older child can add and when.
- Phone technology changes often so stay up-to-date and be tech-savvy. Your child most certainly will be.
- Warn your older child about the dangers and repercussions of taking inappropriate pictures, sending them to others, or posting them online.
- Prohibit phone usage at mealtime, bedtime, during school and study hours, and when talking in person with others. Multitasking is a myth. In reality, a child's brain cannot assimilate information properly while engaged in multiple tasks.
- Help your child develop interpersonal, face-to-face communication skills. Make your home a haven where kids can talk, play games, eat together, and enjoy one another's company.
- Direct your child to write out the phone usage rules, sign them, and post them in a prominent place.

In your daughter's case, upon discovering her second phone misuse, you could confiscate the cell phone indefinitely and reevaluate the pros and cons of her having a phone now that you see she may not have the maturity to use it correctly.

If you decide to withhold phone usage temporarily, set a reasonable time limit and then reinstate her phone privileges with stiffer guidelines and more frequent monitoring. If the problem continues, increase the length of the next restriction.

Refer to chapter 24, "Lying," to address the deception revealed through your child's phone records. If inappropriate photos or text messages have been sent or received, work with the parents of the other children involved to address the problem or block these children's phone numbers.

What Could You Say?

To establish boundaries when you first give your child a phone, you could say, "I'm giving you a cell phone so we can stay connected. Plus, I trust you and believe you're mature enough to make good choices.

"Rules for using this phone will change as you mature and as I see you choosing to use your phone responsibly. Let's review the rules now." [Do so.]

"This cell phone doesn't belong to you. I'm allowing you to *use* it. If you choose to abuse the privilege, you'll also be choosing to lose the use of the phone. If that happens, you'll need to earn it back over time. I trust you and believe you're ready for this next step."

Assuming you had such a conversation with your daughter when you initially gave her a cell phone, now you must have a different conversation after she's broken the rules:

"Having this phone was important to you and to me. When I returned it to you, I was happy for you to have it back—and hopeful you'd choose to follow the rules. But that's not been your choice.

"Your texts and e-mails show you've chosen to be untrustworthy. You've deceived, disobeyed, and disrespected me. This hurt, and it's very disappointing. The phone will stay with me now. You may not borrow a phone, either. Cell phones will be completely off-limits until you have proven you can be trusted. To help you do that, I want you to spend some time making a list of ways you can earn my trust and we will discuss the list next Sunday after lunch."

Later, as your daughter matures and demonstrates increased trustworthiness, you could say, "Let's review the cell phone rules and tell me what you'll do differently the next time you're entrusted with a phone." [Discuss her comments.] Once she has demonstrated readiness for her phone privilege to be restored, you could say, "I'll check regularly to ensure you're making wise choices with the phone. If you choose to break the rules, I'll take your phone for the rest of the school year and we'll try letting you use it again when you're more mature.

"I love you and your safety is very important. Obeying the rules, being trustworthy, and having self-control are important too. The Bible says, 'One who is faithful in a very little is also faithful in much, and one who is dishonest in a very little is also dishonest in much' (Luke 16:10).

"That's how it works with your cell phone. When you choose to use it the right way, you'll be rewarded with more freedom, more phone features, and more talk time!"

Wisdom from God's Word

As cell phone use continues to mushroom among children, be aware that receiving a new phone may test your child's priorities and commitment to love God above a cell phone and to prioritize time with him over time on the phone. What a wonderful opportunity, then, to help your child embrace Luke 10:27: "You shall love the Lord your God with all your heart and with all your soul and with all your strength and with all your mind, and your neighbor as yourself."

See these related chapters:
Chapter 21: "Harmful Habits and Addictions," page 137
Chapter 26: "Media Mania," page 164

13

Cheating

After considerable research, you enroll your daughter in an excellent school. Olivia makes friends, likes her teachers, and surprises you with her improved grades. Problems at the previous school are nothing more than past history. At least that's what you think . . . until today.

You receive a form from Olivia's teacher requesting a conference. *For what?* you wonder, quickly scanning the attached note, searching for clues. Then you see it—a word you would *never* have associated with your little girl: *cheating*.

Olivia's been caught with answers scribbled on her arm. Now her teacher passes the problem to you—along with a stern warning: At this exclusive school, cheating may mean expulsion. Now you grapple with what to do—why on earth would she *cheat*?

What Could You Do?

At its core, cheating often is motivated by the desire to feel increased significance. The best deterrent to cheating, then, is to help your child see her intrinsic value in your eyes and the eyes of God, develop godly character, and find effective study methods that will support scholastic success.

In the case of your daughter caught cheating at school, you could:

- Pray for ears to hear the truth, listen with an open mind, and collect the facts surrounding any and all allegations that your child has cheated.
- Ask your child to share with you her definition of cheating. This will help you discern whether she is intentionally cheating or simply needs instruction regarding what is—and isn't—permissible. Explain that cheating is a form of lying that destroys trust.
- Try to determine *why* your child is cheating.
  - Is she experiencing hearing or vision problems? If so, seek medical care at once.
  - If she feels overly pressured to make good grades, explore your expectations and how best to communicate them.
  - If she's bored and looking for shortcuts, explore ways to make learning more engaging—while explaining that some aspects of life simply aren't fun but they must be completed nonetheless.
  - If she's fallen behind and you're unable to help her catch up, she may need a competent tutor.
- Avoid name-calling and labeling, such as "you're a cheater." Correct the wrong behavior without condemning your child.
- Establish ethical guidelines for completing school assignments. Show your older child how to obtain information from acceptable sources and give credit when it's due.
- Develop a positive partnership with your child's school in order to deal decisively with cheating. If the school doesn't have an honor code, suggest it adopt one.[1] These steps will assure your child that the adults in authority in her life are committed to integrity and to her welfare.
- Though she cheated on schoolwork, assigning additional homework sends the message that homework is a form of punishment. Instead, explain that all learning is beneficial, strengthening and challenging the brain. Even subjects that aren't her favorites can develop her mental faculties.
- Adjust your child's schedule if she needs more time for homework.
- Review all completed homework until the next report card. Help your child prepare for tests by quizzing her beforehand.

- As she continues in school, maintain an open dialogue with your child, encouraging her progress and praising her efforts. Your involvement will help deter future problems.
- Accompany your child to apologize to her teacher.
- If the teacher has established reasonable repercussions for cheating (such as assigning a failing grade to the project), support the teacher.
- With your child, fill two small flowerpots with soil. Let her plant sprouted bean seeds in each pot. Instruct her to water the second pot with bleach. Over the next week, as your child observes the beans growing in the first pot, read, then paraphrase, Galatians 6:7–8: "The Bible says you'll harvest what you plant. When you plant honesty and your best effort, you'll see good results and grow character. Cheating is like poison. It damages the soil of your heart."
- Read the story of Jacob and Esau in Genesis 25:19–34; 27. Jacob and Rebekah cheated the people they loved. What was the result?

What Could You Say?

To help your daughter overcome the temptation to cheat, you could say, "I love you and I'm always proud when I see you studying and giving your best effort. But I'm even more proud when I see you choosing to be honest and trustworthy.

"Let's talk through what happened at school. Tell me about what tempted you to cheat and the reason you decided to do it."

Listen intently to your child's story of the incident. Ask, "How did you feel when you were cheating? Did it make you feel good or bad about yourself?" You could then say, "Cheating is wrong and unfair. It will affect how others think about you and how you think about yourself. After all, how do you feel when you see someone else cheating?" [Listen.] "Teachers, family, and friends will not trust you if you cheat. Ultimately, you will not be able to trust yourself.

"Grades tell us what parts of your subjects you understand and what needs more attention. You risk not getting the help you need if you choose to cheat.

"Being tempted to cheat isn't wrong. Acting on the temptation is wrong. What other choices did you have in that situation? What can you learn from this to help you choose to be honest the next time you're tempted to cheat?"

Listen and commend your child for her worthwhile ideas and add your own suggestions. For instance, "What do you think about . . . [asking for help, giving your best effort even if you don't feel it is good enough, not always being in first place in class, etc.]? Learning to handle these feelings is part of life and growing up.

"Cheating is a problem that only you can choose to fix. For a time, you will not watch television or movies. This will give you more time to focus on your schoolwork. If you're having trouble with a subject, please ask for help from your teacher or from me.

"God's Word says, 'When someone has been given much, much will be required in return' (Luke 12:48 NLT) and 'whoever knows the right thing to do and fails to do it, for him it is sin' (James 4:17). You've been given a wonderful mind, and you know cheating is wrong. Part of the 'much' God requires is that you succeed in school by being responsible in doing your homework and learning the subject matter. Then you can know you have earned whatever grade you make and feel good about it without cheating. Your teachers and I are here to help you do that.

"I love you, no matter what grades you make, and so does God!"

Wisdom from God's Word

Integrity is a character trait we choose daily. The Bible says, "The integrity of the upright guides them, but the crookedness of the treacherous destroys them" (Prov. 11:3). Temptations to lie, cheat, or steal perpetually arise. We would be wise to teach our children to pray every day, "Teach me your way, O LORD, that I may walk in your truth" (Ps. 86:11).

See these related chapters:
Chapter 22: "Homework Hassles," page 143
Chapter 24: "Lying," page 152

14

Chores

About to put away a dirty cup, you discover the dishwasher has not been unloaded. Not only is this posted on the chore chart for your daughter, Emma, but you reminded her about it just an hour ago. You realize a pattern is developing as you recall that she disappeared for long periods of time when the family cleaned the garage and again when everyone unpacked from vacation.

Glancing out the window, you see Emma playing with her brother, who has already completed his daily chores. You wonder, *Wouldn't it be easier to do it myself and avoid the inevitable confrontation?* Well . . . *would it?*

What Is a Work Ethic?

The concept of work and a strong work ethic began when God placed Adam in the garden and told him to "work it and keep it" (Gen. 2:15). God never intended for human beings to be idle. After Adam sinned, however, God said, "By the sweat of your face you shall eat bread" (Gen. 3:19). Work became toilsome, but God didn't remove the rewards of enjoying the "fruits" of our labor.

In 2 Thessalonians 3:6–12, Paul is emphatic: When someone does not work, it is considered to be "disorderly" (KJV), contrary to our human nature. "If anyone is not willing to work, let him not eat. For we hear that some among you walk in idleness, not busy at work, but busybodies. Now such persons we command and encourage in the Lord Jesus Christ to do their work quietly and to earn their own living." Obviously, Paul was addressing adults. However, cultivating a well-developed work ethic should begin in childhood.

Why Should Children Learn at Home to Work?

Some parents believe it isn't right to require children to perform household chores. Perhaps there doesn't seem to be enough time or it is simply easier to do the work themselves. Whatever the reason, if children do not learn to do their fair share at home, they are being deprived of one of life's most valuable lessons.

God created the home as the foundation of civilization. Children gain confidence and satisfaction from choosing to contribute to the family. Traditionally, children who learn to work under the loving tutelage of parents fare better in academics, sports, music, and relationships.[1] These children experience rewards for their efforts and know the satisfaction of a job well done. Cultivating a strong work ethic helps build self-worth and teaches interdependence, preparing children to one day make positive contributions to their communities as adults.

What Could You Do?

Encourage personal responsibility while your child is young. If you begin with simple jobs, even little children can participate. Your role is to organize, instruct, delegate, monitor, inspect, coach, and encourage your children as they become increasingly adept at performing tasks on their own. To get started:

- Set up a chore chart, breaking tasks into component steps for younger children. Chore charts allow children to take individual ownership of their tasks.
- Assign chores pertinent to each individual child (such as, put away your own toys) as well as age-appropriate chores that benefit the entire family (like help put away the dishes after meals). At the beginning of each week, rotate family-related chores. If

your child has done a poor job or has required much reminding, she may need to do that chore for a second week.

- Along with each chore, assign a designated time for completion (before school, after dinner, before playtime, etc.).
- At a family meeting, explain how your household chore system will work. Have children repeat back what they've heard.
- Invite your children to share their ideas on what chores they can assume. Brainstorm how these could best be accomplished in light of school and study schedules. Collaboration encourages your child to take ownership and become accountable.
- Post the chore chart where everyone can see it. For little ones who do not yet read, make pictures of the expected task. For example, a drawing of a bed reminds your younger child to make the bed.
- Practice using the chore chart together until you know that each child is familiar with the process. After that, refrain from reminding—let the chart do its job.
- Coach young children through the chore process until they are old enough to do their part with minimal assistance. Placing stickers next to each completed job provides visual reinforcement.
- Don't assume your child has mastered a skill until you see it demonstrated. Apply the adage popularized in business: "You can expect what you inspect."
- Tell your children, "I expect your best effort." If their work doesn't match their capabilities, insist that it be redone. "Do not let your hands be weak, for your work shall be rewarded" (2 Chron. 15:7).
- Avoid redoing your children's work *when they've done their best*. Otherwise, it will be demoralizing and communicate "your best isn't good enough." Assign age-appropriate tasks, teach incrementally, and require only what is appropriate for your child's ability.
- Teach gently and affirm your child for a job well done.
- Whenever possible, make work fun or even into a game.
- Create a "Joy Jar" from which your child has the privilege of selecting a new task at a special occasion, such as a birthday along with a new privilege (e.g., extended bedtime). Celebrate

this as a rite of passage. Instead of chores being a "have-to," they can become viewed as an honor and a sign of growing up.

Here are examples of specific tasks, by age group:

Ages Two and Three

- Help make their bed. Use a comforter that is easy to move.
- Make a clothing selection from two outfits you pick out. This teaches your child to choose, but you still limit the choices.
- Get dressed independently. Help only with buttons, zippers, or laces that are too difficult for little fingers. To minimize toileting accidents, provide clothes that can easily be slipped on and off without adult help.
- Help brush their own hair.
- Help brush teeth. (Initially, have your child give you the toothbrush after finishing so you can quickly brush missed places.)
- Fold small laundry items like washcloths, hand towels, and underwear.
- Put away clothes.
- Put away toys.
- Help set silverware on the table.
- Help clear table after a meal (remove napkins, trash, light items).
- Help with simple food preparation, such as stirring and mixing.

Ages Four and Five

- Dust furniture.
- Wipe doorknobs.
- Vacuum small areas with lightweight dust buster.
- Sweep small areas with small broom.
- Clean bathroom sinks.
- Help sort drawers and closets.
- Help care for a pet.
- Help put away groceries.
- Help wash and dry dishes. Put away silverware.
- Help make thank-you notes and birthday cards.
- Select clothes to wear (with your final okay).
- Help pack for an overnight stay away from home.

• Help with simple food preparation—make peanut butter and jelly sandwich, pour cereal.

Ages Six and Seven

• Empty dishwasher, put away whatever can be easily reached.
• Remember to return library book.
• Clean out car.
• Empty small wastebaskets into trash containers.
• Practice music lessons.
• Write thank-you notes for gifts received.
• Sweep sidewalk.
• Rake leaves.
• Take shower or bath and wash own hair.
• Help pack school lunches.
• Help plan and prepare one family meal per week (with adult supervision).
• Vacuum own bedroom.
• Fold and put away laundry.

Ages Eight and Nine

• Vacuum several rooms.
• Clean own bedroom.
• Perform simple sewing and mending.
• Make simple repairs, such as using a hammer and nail.
• Help decorate their bedroom.
• Clean inside and outside of car with adult supervision.
• Occasionally help plan, shop for, prepare, and clean up after a simple meal.
• Do simple loads of laundry.
• Learn to budget an allowance (see chap. 27 "Money and Materialism" on p. 170).
• Clean mirrors and easy-to-reach windows.

Ages Ten to Twelve

• Care for personal clothing.
• Organize own bedroom and desk (assuming you've already taught basic organization skills). Consistently allow your child's

individual personality to come through, even if methods and tastes differ from yours.

- Bake something by following a recipe.
- Earn money by completing extra chores.
- Learn to budget and manage money.
- Occasionally help plan and shop for a simple meal—prepare it and clean up afterward.
- Change bedding.
- Learn to define, write out, and arrange the steps to accomplish a goal.
- Mow yard.
- Plan and organize simple special event.

Now, back to your daughter who keeps dodging chores. Ask her to please come inside. Standing near the full dishwasher, share your concern that she has been repeatedly choosing to neglect her duties. Consequently, because she chose not to empty the dishwasher earlier, she will need to wash a load of dishes by hand. In addition, instead of rotating to another chore, unloading the dishwasher will need to remain as her chore for the next week and every week thereafter until she masters this task.

What Could You Say?

In the case of your daughter, you could say, "I appreciate how you enjoy playing with your brother. But being a part of our family means we love each other by serving each other as well as by playing with each other.

"The Bible says in Galatians 5:13, 'Through love serve one another.' Whose job is it to unload the dishwasher?" [Wait for the correct answer.] "When you choose not to do your chores, you're choosing not to serve. That isn't fair. It makes extra work for someone else in the family.

"Today your brother chose to do his chores so he could go out and play. My heart's desire is that you too realize that *playtime is a reward* for doing your chores, *not a right*."

While washing dishes that evening, if your daughter complains, you could calmly say, "Honey, you could choose to look at this job as a way of expressing your love for your family, not as a punishment. That way, you will be doing it with a positive attitude. Remember our rule: *'Choosing to do a chore with a poor attitude means choosing to do extra work'*—like sweeping the floor. I know you don't want that. I don't want that for you either. I much prefer you doing your work as if you were doing it for God . . . because you *are!*"

Inspect the work when it is complete. If it is performed according to your child's age and skill level, tell her, "Well done! I'm proud of you! Thank you." If she did a poor job, you could say, "Let's try this again to see if you can improve on it."

Be sure to encourage your child along the way. "I can see you're working hard to make sure our family has clean dishes. Thanks for serving us, honey, and especially for doing it with a loving attitude."

Wisdom from God's Word

Children are most teachable when they are young. Therefore, train your child to enjoy the benefits of work during this teachable time so they *want* to help and consider it a joy.

Tell your child: "If you tuck this verse inside your heart for the rest of your life, you will always have a good attitude about work and you'll see it as a privilege . . . and it is! The Bible says, 'Whatever you are doing, work at it with enthusiasm, as to the Lord and not for people' (Col. 3:23 NET)."

See Chapter 31: "Procrastination," page 191

15

Cliques

Several mothers report that your daughter, Ashley, has created a type of "caste system" at school based on the cost of clothing and certain accessories worn by each girl in her class. Those who don't measure up are excluded from conversations, recreation, and social invitations.

The revelation that your little "fashionista" is manipulating and excluding her peers makes you feel angry, hurt, embarrassed, and sad. *How could Ashley become this kind of . . . snob? And now what do you do?*

Why Cliques?

A clique is "a small group of people who spend time together and who are not friendly to other people."[1] Cliques are not the same as interest-based groups and clubs. To gain acceptance and develop their social world, children often gravitate toward groups and clubs based on common interests. While most youth organizations function on a set of clearly defined rules, cliques are based on power, manipulation, prejudice, and exclusivity. Acceptance comes with a price: an unspoken vow to uphold the clique's unfair practices and unbalanced power structure.

Often, cliques are controlled by mean-spirited power brokers. Victims may be "in" with the clique one day and "out" the next, without knowing the real reason why. Children excluded by cliques typically can feel insecure, demeaned, and isolated.

What Could You Do?

Nearly every school—public and private—has problems with cliques. Here are ideas for breaking up a snobbish clan in your child's world:

- Lead by personal example. Interact with others beyond your own social circle and include your child when possible. Don't judge others based on their skin color, professions, possessions, or other external factors. Treat all people with respect and dignity regardless of whether they are "like you" or not.
- Provide an emotionally safe, peaceful haven for your child to authentically express questions, cares, and concerns. Establish times when your child can talk with you freely. This can be during a shared meal, driving to or from school, helping with homework, doing the dishes, or before bedtime.
- Create an environment into which your child feels comfortable bringing friends home. Get to know these friends and watch how your child interacts with them.
- Acknowledge that your child has a need to fit in and be accepted as a part of something bigger than herself. Help her see that when her values are out of order, she may seek her worth from "things" rather than from her identity in Christ. Equip her with these truths:
  - Groups and friends often change, but God never will (Heb. 13:8).
  - Cliques do not define who you are (Eph. 2:10), but God does (1 John 3:11).
- Help your child develop the kind of strong character that can change the dynamics of a social group from the *inside out*. A biblical view of self-worth, confidence, and empathy—and the values of diversity, inclusion, and friendliness—will go far in guarding against a clique mentality.[2]
- Patiently explore the false beliefs at the core of assigning worth based on outward appearances. Through prayer, perseverance,

and involvement, you can provide the trust and emotional safety your child will need in order to identify and correct her false beliefs.

    – Role-playing, humor, exaggerated examples, and games can help your child drop defenses.

- Use biblical principles such as the Golden Rule (Luke 6:31) and the biblical confrontation model in Matthew 18 to teach your child how to relate to others in a Christlike manner. Explain the difference between exercising biblical discernment and having a critical, judgmental spirit. Share with your child James 2:1–10, a compelling condemnation of partiality.

- Encourage your child to visit and interact with different groups of peers each week. More than likely, new friendships will form and petty divisions will no longer matter.

- Be present at your child's activities. Occasionally stop in at school for a pleasant surprise visit, bring lunch, sit in on a class, observe an athletic practice, watch a rehearsal, or pick up your child from school for an unexpected outing. Be a participating parent who provides transportation to activities and events, supplies refreshments, coaches sports teams, or assists the organization's leader. These steps will enable you to witness your child interacting with peers and encourage positive leadership skills.

- Read Acts 2:42–47 together and compare how your child's friends treat others with how these early Christians behaved.

- Help your child to develop a heart for serving others less fortunate, such as volunteering at an inner-city ministry, a home for the elderly, a shelter for abused children . . . and especially a church missions trip.

- Find activities that will boost your child's confidence. From raising rabbits to playing the piano, from collecting "collectibles" to cooking casseroles, cookies, and cakes—being good at something strengthens confidence and makes a child less susceptible to a clique mentality.

- Proverbs 13:20 says, "Whoever walks with the wise becomes wise." The best insurance against the power of cliques is the caliber of friends in your child's life. Help your daughter know what to look for in a true friend.

- Exclude your child from any activities and groups that pointedly promote cliquishness.

- Organize a team or group to teach children how to lead in healthy ways and to implement policies and procedures to eliminate cliques.

- Schools requiring a dress code with uniforms attempt to "level the playing field" in regard to clothing. But children can still find ways to perpetuate cliques by excluding those who don't have pricey accessories or expensive electronic devices. Therefore, you might:
  - Require your child to earn money for accessories during the coming school semester.
  - Shop at stores that do not have high-priced labels.

- With effective adult involvement, a clique's leader can be a powerful force for positive change. Ringleaders typically hide their own fears and insecurities by playing power games. Once their defensive walls crumble, others often will continue to follow, but in a positive direction.
  - When there is true repentance, a caring adult should be on hand immediately to demonstrate love and forgiveness. Rather than condemnation, show how to seek restitution and restoration.

What Could You Say?

In the case of your daughter, the ringleader of a school-based clique, you could say, "I met with your teacher and the principal today because cliques are a problem at your school and they've asked for my help. Now I'm asking for yours. Tell me, what is a clique and what do you think about them?" [Listen carefully to see if she'll open up.]

If she doesn't, gently continue, "As much as it hurts me, I think *you* are part of a clique. You've started valuing others based on what you think their clothes are worth rather than on who they are

as individuals. Please help me understand your reasons for that."
[Listen to her reply.] "This breaks my heart . . . and God's, too.

"The Bible says, 'Man looks on the outward appearance but the
Lord looks on the heart' (1 Sam. 16:7). If you measure a person's
worth by appearance, you'll be wrong every time.

"I've been thinking about an area of giftedness that you have.
Starting a clique and convincing your friends to join shows me that
God has blessed you with leadership skills. This marvelous gift can
be greatly used by God to bless others. I'm giving you a choice of
several clubs to learn about leadership skills and after you join one,
your leadership skills can grow even more.

"You'll also begin doing volunteer work with me every month
at the downtown homeless shelter. I'll be praying that as you serve
people who don't have as much as you, you'll develop a compassion for their pain and their problems—just as God cares for
yours.

"Meanwhile, for the rest of the school year, you'll need to earn
money or save your allowance for any new clothes or accessories.
This will help you see that money and things aren't nearly as important as seeing people the way God sees them.

"As for the girls in your class that you've hurt: You're going
to invite them over next weekend to spend the night. Their moms
already have given them permission to come. This will help you get
to know them. After that, you'll make a card for each girl, saying
three things you appreciate about each one—ways God made each
girl special as a *person*.

"Until the cards have been delivered, you won't spend time with
your other girlfriends after school or on weekends. This will help
you focus on getting to know the girls you've been excluding. Your
reward will be gaining new friends and relationships based on what
really matters.

"I want to hear your ideas on how to make things right with
the girls you left out of your clique. I love you, and I know you
can choose to treat others—no matter who they are—in a way that

honors God. I'm hopeful about how God is going to use this situation to help you be more like him."

Wisdom from God's Word

Judging others based on outward appearances is the foundation of cliques and is in direct opposition to how our God of grace looks at us. Grace means undeserved, unmerited care. God's Word tells us that each of us has value. James 2:1–4 reminds us, "My dear brothers and sisters, how can you claim to have faith in our glorious Lord Jesus Christ if you favor some people over others? For example, suppose someone comes into your meeting dressed in fancy clothes and expensive jewelry, and another comes in who is poor and dressed in dirty clothes. If you give special attention and a good seat to the rich person, but you say to the poor one, 'You can stand over there, or else sit on the floor'—well, doesn't this discrimination show that your judgments are guided by evil motives?" (NLT).

See Chapter 10: "Bullying," page 79

16

Clothing Clashes

Your daughter, Heather, spent the afternoon at a friend's house before meeting you at your son's basketball game. When she strolls in courtside, you try not to stare. Her peers, however, especially the boys, aren't as subtle. Are those shorts—or four scraps of faded denim laced together? And where did she get that tight-fitting tank top?

Meanwhile, Heather is all smiles, drawing numerous glances that stroke her youthful ego. Later, you learn she'd gone shopping that afternoon with a girlfriend and her older sister.

You've covered what is—and isn't—acceptable clothing with Heather before. Now it's her turn to cover . . . *up*!

What Could You Do?

Kids tend to think differently about clothing depending on their age. It's likely a preschool child is exercising independence when resisting clothing choices, whereas an older child is more likely seeking peer acceptance, attention, and admiration.

Clothing can provide insight into your child's heart, so pay attention to her choices. Ask God to help you look beyond the exterior to the interior motive. Proverbs 14:8 says, "The wisdom of the prudent is to discern his way, but the folly of fools is deceiving."

In addition, you could:

- Clearly define what standards your entire family will uphold regarding clothing, and why. This helps ensure that no individual family member feels "picked on."
- Explain that you, too, follow a dress code—whether at work, at jury duty, at church—wherever. As a parent, dress modestly and age-appropriately—even at home. You are responsible for setting an example.
- Starting between the ages of three and five, allow your child to select her daily outfit from a few options you've preselected.
- Early on, have casual conversations about why certain clothing styles are preferable over others.
- Say *yes* to your child's wardrobe choices as often as possible, even when color combinations and patterns aren't ones you prefer.
  - Rigidity in the area of clothing is a recipe for problems, so allow flexibility for self-expression—but always within the confines of modesty and decency.
  - Require older children of both genders to wear a shirt around the house.
- Praise your child for making good choices and continue giving her more shopping autonomy as she demonstrates ongoing good judgment. Likewise, gently rein in choices that veer in the wrong direction.
- When your older child is permitted to shop with a friend or another family member, make sure that clothing rules are clearly communicated and understood. If purchased clothing doesn't meet the standards, help your child return the item to the store and select something more suitable.
- Teach your child how to properly care for her clothes—how to do laundry and how to iron.

For Girls

It has become increasingly challenging to find clothes for girls that don't send an overt or implied sensual message. As you work with your daughter:

- Explore the meaning of 1 Timothy 2:9–10, "Women should adorn themselves in respectable apparel, with modesty and self-control . . . with what is proper for women who profess godliness—with good works."
- Assure her that you are eager to help her dress so she feels confident and attractive, and so she presents herself with dignity and self-respect. Encourage her creativity. For example, layer favorite pieces that don't cover enough with other pieces that do.
- Remind your daughter that certain types of clothing draw inappropriate attention and distract people from being drawn to her beautiful Christlike character.
- Teach her this modesty test: In front of a full-length mirror, bend over, sit, squat, and cross her legs. The outfit passes the test when your child can do these common movements and remain covered.
- Fathers: Praise your daughter's appropriate clothing choices and inward beauty.
  - As she internalizes how her clothing and character encourage respectful treatment, she will be less likely to settle for disrespect from young men.
  - When a nurturing father-daughter relationship is nonexistent, a grandfather, uncle, or other father figure can fill this role.

For Boys

Like girls, boys often seek attention through their clothing or lack thereof. Consider these guidelines:

- Require good hygiene and clean clothes as an everyday standard.
- Allow "sloppy favorites"—as long as they're clean—for around the house, for play, and for sports practice. But require nicer clothes for other settings.
- Remove tattered items from your son's wardrobe.
- Prohibit clothing bearing inappropriate wording or graphics and ill-fitted pants that hang well below the waist.

Now back to your daughter who arrived at the basketball game in a newly acquired outfit that was clearly off-limits. Here are ideas to help her learn from her poor choice:

- Intercept your daughter and gently and discreetly redirect her out the nearest exit. Once you're alone together, tell her that her new outfit is inappropriate.
  - Either take her home to change clothes, or
  - If you can't take her home, find a wrap, jacket, or another item of clothing to cover her while she sits next to you until the game ends.
- If the clothing she wore to the game was borrowed, return it. If it was purchased, it can't be returned, so it will need to be donated or discarded.
  - Explain that since your daughter chose not to follow the rules, you will not supply funds to replace these items. As a result, she will have fewer pieces in her wardrobe.
- Tell your daughter that you will begin accompanying her on all clothes shopping trips until she demonstrates she is able to make better choices. When her choices reflect good judgment, reward her with greater autonomy.
  - Once your daughter has earned the right to shop for clothing without you, stipulate that until further notice, she must get your approval *before* making a purchase (e.g., she could send you a cell phone photo). If you're unavailable, your daughter is not to wear an outfit or remove the tags until you've approved it. The Bible says, "Let there be no sexual immorality, impurity, or greed among you. Such sins have no place among God's people" (Eph. 5:3 NLT).

What Could You Say?

Your daughter's behavior likely is driven by a need to be noticed and approved, so affirm her intrinsic worth. "Honey, you're beautiful inside and out, and so very special to God and to me. I love your unique creativity and fashion flair.

"Lately, though, your clothing choices haven't reflected good judgment. Clothing choices can say a lot about a person. Your clothes should fit so that you can move easily with style and modesty." [Review the meaning of *modesty* if necessary.] "When what you wear isn't modest, you *do* get attention, but not the kind of attention that honors you or God.

"You want people to admire you based on who you are and how you behave, not because of how much of your body you're willing to show them. When you respect yourself, others are also more likely to respect you too.

"I'll help you choose clothes that you like and that meet our family standards. While you're learning to make good clothing choices, I'll have the final say.

"As a reward for dressing modestly, I'll gradually give you more freedom to select your own outfits—ones with your special stamp of creativity. We'll even plan a shopping trip just for the two of us."

Wisdom from God's Word

From the time they are very young, help your children understand the priority of inner attractiveness. Colossians 3:12 describes how we are to clothe ourselves spiritually . . . which will protect us in every other area of our lives: "As God's chosen people holy and dearly loved, clothe yourself with compassion, kindness, humility, gentleness and patience" (NIV).

See these related chapters:
Chapter 30: "Peer Pressure," page 186
Chapter 34: "Sexual Storms," page 204

Disrespectfulness

In early childhood, your son, Sam, was as close as a boy could be to you. Then, a week ago, he looked directly into your eyes and said, "Shut up! You don't know anything! You're so stupid."

You still haven't recovered. You were so shocked, you neglected to discipline him.

You saw such anger in his eyes that a part of you became fearful—afraid of more venom from your formerly sweet ten-year-old.

You hoped Sam would feel remorse and eventually apologize. Unfortunately, this hasn't happened. Now you're wondering when he might lash out again.

What Could You Do?

Developmentally, children go through argumentative phases. Two-year-olds may stomp their feet to assert their will. Children ages ten to twelve explore independence by exhibiting a heightened need to debate, dialogue, and dispute. Suddenly the same parent, who was the brilliant center of the child's universe last week, now knows next to nothing. It's a daunting moment for even the strongest parent. After all, few things hurt a parent's heart more than disrespect from their own flesh and blood. But when it comes—especially the first time—it has the power of a stun gun.

Left unchecked, disrespect will only grow worse, so you must teach your child to work through hostile feelings in a godly way, "and in your teaching show integrity, dignity, and sound speech" (Titus 2:7–8).

So consider this practical plan of action:

- As soon as possible, talk with your son about what happened and how you felt. If he's unable to communicate respectfully, send him to his room until he chooses to express himself constructively.
- Remember, you're dealing with a child, so don't overly burden him with the responsibility for your emotions. But make it clear: Disrespect will not be tolerated.
- Give your son the opportunity to respond. Ask him to repeat what he said and then help him explore what he felt. Many children (adults, too) struggle to name their feelings. A chart that enables your child to pick a face that shows what he's feeling can help. Find sample charts online by searching for "children's play therapy feelings chart."
- After listening, affirm that you love him and that neither you nor God want to see his heart remain disrespectful. Proverbs 15:1 says, "A soft answer turns away wrath, but a harsh word stirs up anger."
- Role-play respectful ways to express strong emotions.
- For a younger child, have him "hold his tongue"—literally— when his tone and words are disrespectful. That is, have him stick out his tongue and hold it between his thumb and fingers.[1] Unconventional? Yes. But it may help him remember this biblical lesson: "Whoever derides their neighbor has no sense, but the one who has understanding holds their tongue" (Prov. 11:12 NIV).
- You may wish to allow a "redo." That is, instruct your child to leave the room, take a deep breath, come back in, and respond with genuine respect.[2]
- Let your child know that in the future, he may record or write about any grievances he has and present these to you, along with his ideas about possible *solutions* and how he can *contrib-*

ute to those solutions. Tell your child you'll choose to hear him out when he chooses to communicate respectfully.

- Require an in-person apology and explain to your child that until he apologizes, his every request will be denied.
  - If your child begins making requests of you before choosing to sincerely apologize, say an immediate *no* to his requests, without entertaining discussion. When he asks why you're suddenly denying him, tell him to go to his room and think about it and then let you know when he has ideas to discuss.
  - Most children will realize their own poor attitude is the problem and then apologize. Accept your child's sincere apology, but don't reverse your earlier refusals. Doing so teaches your child to make empty apologies simply to manipulate you.[3]
- In the future, when his words are meant to hurt, remove your child's privilege to speak for a predetermined amount of time.
- Ask your child to memorize: "Love is patient and kind; love does not envy or boast, it is not arrogant or rude" (1 Cor. 13:5–6).
- Consider, are there other areas where you are tolerating your child's disrespect? For example, if he's is in the habit of calling out to you from another room, unless it is an emergency, don't respond. This will train your child to talk *to* you . . . not *at* you.

What Could You Say?

In the case of your disrespectful child, you could say, "Son, I love you with all my heart, and I'm glad you know you can come to me about whatever concerns you. But when you shouted at me to shut up and called me stupid, your words hurt me deeply. I'm very concerned about the anger and disrespect I saw in your eyes and heard in your voice.

"Instead, you're to speak to me respectfully at *all* times—even when you're angry and upset. Yet how did you speak to me?" [Wait for his reply.] "When you chose to disrespect me, you also chose the consequences: not talking on the phone for the rest of the week, and being grounded this weekend. I've picked up a book about a person with a respectful heart. You'll spend the weekend reading this book. You'll also write about what you learned and make a list of ways you're going to show me more respect.

"I also expect a sincere apology. The Bible says to honor your father and mother (this is the first commandment with a promise), that things will go well with you.

"If you feel angry about something someone has done, but don't know a respectful way to say it, let me know. I'll help you practice respectful ways to use your words to say what's in your heart. When we work together like this, you'll feel heard . . . and others will feel respected."

Wisdom from God's Word

A heart of respect is best trained and nurtured early—and at home. The Bible says in Proverbs 1:8, "Listen, my son, to your father's instruction and do not forsake your mother's teaching," and in Proverbs 12:1, "Whoever loves discipline loves knowledge and whoever hates correction is stupid" (NIV).

See these related chapters:

Disrupting Class

The phone call is from your child's teacher. This is the third time he's talked to you about your daughter, Jessica, disrupting class. Previous calls were because she would interrupt the teacher's lesson. But this time, when a student answered the teacher's question, Jessica jumped up and ridiculed the other child. Embarrassed, the classmate broke out in tears.

Not only are these disruptions interfering with instruction, but Jessica's actions are hurting others. She *must* stop this unacceptable behavior now. But how?

Why Do Kids Disrupt Class?

Though there are many reasons a child may disrupt class, here are some of the more common ones:

- If a child's private life is tumultuous, unpredictable, and out of control, she may attempt to control her classroom.
- Convinced she isn't smart, a child may give up academically and instead grasp for peer approval by becoming the class clown. (This may bring the added bonus of dissuading the teacher from calling on her in class.)
- An "I'm right and everyone else is wrong" attitude may stem from immaturity, perfectionism, and/or just plain self-centeredness.

- Underchallenged, a bright student may disrupt out of sheer boredom.
- An insecure child may seek to prove she's smart by proving she's *right*.
- A child who's frequently inattentive, hyperactive, and impulsive—to a greater degree than her peers and for six months or longer—may have ADHD.[1]

What Could You Do?

- Try to determine the motivation behind your child's behavior. Is she disruptive and impulsive at home or only at school?
- If your child's teacher has established class rules, get a copy and review them with your child. Post the rules near her study area at home.
- Determine a firm, appropriate boundary with the help of your child's teacher, school counselor, and principal. For example, if your child disrupts, she will miss recess and stay in the classroom to complete teacher-assigned tasks.
- Help your child recognize her strengths and award positive feedback for academic *effort*, not just ability. Children yearn for attention and approval. If they can't get it for positive behavior, they'll get it for negative behavior. Affirming your child's efforts encourages concentration on the task at hand rather than on making others laugh.
- Help your attention-seeking child find productive uses for her talents and abilities. Provide opportunities through church youth groups, scouts, music, drama, sports, or other activities for which she shows aptitude and interest.
- Help your child distinguish between black, white, and gray areas in life. Make a game of describing situations while your child decides if it is an issue of right, wrong, or a matter of opinion.
- On a calendar, award a star each day the teacher doesn't report an "interrupting" day. Celebrate the first successful day, the first week, and your child's graduation after a month.
- A sense of humor is a valuable characteristic to be encouraged. If your child is gifted with natural wit:

- Talk with her about when it's appropriate to use humor and when it's time to remain quiet (especially when someone else—such as a teacher—is speaking).
- Consider involving her in organized activities that welcome humor and offer participants the opportunity to perform in front of groups.
• Help your child find ways to expend excess energy through regular physical activity such as dance or sports.
• With the teacher's permission, join your child in class for a day to monitor her behavior. Or, if your schedule doesn't permit it, have a respected adult substitute for you.
- A variation: Monitor your child's behavior from the hallway, *outside* the open classroom door. Stand discreetly out of view. Instruct the teacher to send your child into the hallway when she acts out. There, calmly but firmly correct her misbehavior. Let her know she'll be choosing to forfeit a favorite activity whenever she disrupts and that, periodically, you'll be making more surprise visits.
- If you suspect ADHD, have your child professionally screened.[2]

In the case of your daughter, whose frequent interruptions made a child cry in class, you could also require her to write an apology to the child and their teacher.

What Could You Say?

For the child described in the opening scenario, you could say, "You have many interesting things to say. Honey, I like it when you share your ideas with me. But I got another call from your teacher about you disrupting class. I'd like to know what happened." [Listen carefully, amplifying as needed.]

"Some things are either right or wrong. God tells us in the Bible that stealing is wrong. But many other things are a matter of opinion. For instance, you like riding a skateboard and I like riding a bike. Neither one of us is wrong. Both of us are right. We simply prefer different things.

"If you think your teacher or a classmate is wrong, raise your hand and share your thoughts respectfully when you're called on. Or talk with your teacher or me about it after class. But it's wrong to interrupt the class because you disagree with something someone's said.

"Tonight you'll write a note to your classmate, to apologize for interrupting in class today and to ask for forgiveness. You'll also write a note apologizing to your teacher."

If control appears to be a driving force behind your child's disruption, you could say, "Some things in life you can control—like how your desk is organized. But in the classroom, your *teacher* is in control. School needs to be a safe place for students to make mistakes and learn. Trust your teacher to guide you and the class step by step. If you have a problem with your teacher, share it with me after school.

"Now I'd like to hear your thoughts about how you can stop disrupting class." [Listen intently.]

"I've made a calendar so we can track your progress. Your teacher will tell me each day when you've chosen to disrupt. The first day you don't disrupt, you'll get a special surprise. After a week of choosing not to disrupt, you'll get to pick the menu for dinner that night. After a month of not disrupting, we'll celebrate with a trip to the zoo."

If your child disrupts class to gain peer approval, you could say, "You have a great sense of humor. And I know it's fun to make other people laugh, but there's a time to joke and a time to be quiet. During class is the time to listen to your teacher and speak only when called on. Disrupting the class disrespects your teacher and keeps the other kids from learning.

"The reward for choosing to pay attention in class is learning all you can and being known as respectful. From now on if you choose to disrupt, you'll also be choosing to be separated from your friends during class . . . and to stay inside during recess. I doubt you want that, and I don't want it for you. So concentrate on your work during class and save the jokes for later."

Wisdom from God's Word

James 1:19 says, "Let every person be quick to hear, slow to speak, slow to anger." A disruptive tongue does not listen to any voice but its own. Disrupting shows disrespect for what others have to say and especially disrespect for people in positions of authority. This is why understanding biblical principles for everyday problems is so helpful.

See Chapter 23: "Interrupting," page 148

Forgetfulness

"Quick! Answer your phone!" your son, Freddie, pleads frantically into your voicemail. "I left my backpack at home. My homework and lunch are in there. I need you to bring it to school. Ya gotta hurry!"

Freddie's message would have been easier to listen to had he not "forgotten" to use a few niceties . . . like *please*! How many times have you driven home to "save the day," retrieving your son's backpack and shuttling it to his school? Yep, eight times this semester. Will today be the ninth?

Why Do Children Forget?

Do you have a Forgetful Freddie in your family—a child who, despite repeated reminders still manages to leave home without his lunch, homework, gym clothes, or (fill in the blank)? Why is he so forgetful?

- It may simply be a matter of age and maturity. A child's ability to undertake increasingly complex routines and responsibilities naturally improves as his brain develops.
- He may be engaged in a power struggle with you and/or his teachers, not wanting to comply. So he conveniently "forgets."
- Your home may lack structure and a clear organizational system that serves as a reminder for him to gather his belongings.

- It may simply be a bad habit.
- Remembering may not be important to him. If he knows you'll rescue him and that there will be no consequence when he forgets, why try harder?

Often, forgetting is a choice. A child may directly disobey instructions and claim, "I forgot." Consistent boundaries and repercussions help develop neural pathways in the brain and transform the heart with positive character traits.[1]

Natural repercussions—such as missing a meal that's been left in a forgotten lunch bag or getting a failing grade on a homework assignment that didn't make it to class—also help teach children that they are accountable for their actions. However, research shows that for some children, the executive function in the brain—the prefrontal cortex—is slower to develop. This area handles details including remembering, anticipating, organizing, and impulse control. Think of it as the command center or administrative office in your child's brain.

Most of us have experienced going into a room only to discover we don't have a clue why we are there. If someone said in a condescending tone, "What do you mean you can't remember? Did you remember before you went in there? Why can't you remember now?" Would that help? Of course not!

The same is true with children and their developing brains. When a child forgets, it can be because the chemical that makes the neurotransmitter connections operate is not functioning at its full potential. When you walked into a room and forgot why you were there, for a split second your brain's neurotransmitters did not connect. With children, especially those who have neurological disorders (such as ADHD), this can occur more frequently.[2]

What Could You Do?

- Be sympathetic but do not enable or rescue. Establish boundaries that do not include regular shuttle service to deliver forgotten items to your child. It may be hard to reject his repeated requests but natural consequences are often the best teachers. "Do not be deceived: God is not mocked, for whatever one sows, that will he also reap" (Gal. 6:7).

- Consider: What is the worst that can happen? He gets a zero for no homework and feels hungry during lunch? If so, his life is not in danger, nor will he flunk out of school.

- As he goes through school, he will be in much more serious academic trouble if he doesn't learn from these consequences now.

- Equip your child with strategies to help him remember key routines at specific times. For example:

  - Establish a sequence that he can do daily, such as hang up his coat, put his backpack near the door, take his lunch box to the kitchen, and place his schoolwork where he does his homework. Before bed, he puts completed homework in his backpack. In the morning, he adds his lunch to the backpack, and it's ready for school.

  - Help your child rehearse the new routine.

  - Tailor these new strategies to work for your child's individual personality, capacity, and learning style. (See chap. 22 "Homework Hassels" on p. 143 for more on learning styles.) For example, if your child is a visual learner, have him write his assignments in a notebook and check them off when he's done.

  - Practice. Repetition increases proficiency until patterns are ingrained in the brain. Encourage the same routine each day.

- Praise your child for being persistent.

  - As he learns to do the same steps every day, let him know that you are proud of him for remembering.

  - Point out the positives, including his growing sense of accomplishment, decreased stress, and his requirement for less supervision.

- Pray with your child, asking God to help him remember the things in his life that will help him be more responsible, bring him gladness, and give God glory.
- If these steps and others you try don't improve your child's behavior—if he's still frequently forgetful to a greater degree than his peers and it continues for six months or longer—enlist a professional to screen for ADHD, unresolved trauma, or extreme stress.[3] Any of these conditions can contribute to ongoing forgetfulness.

What Could You Say?

In the case of your son, whose call for delivery service you ultimately ignored, you can talk about what happened when you pick him up from school. "Honey, tell me how your day went at school without your backpack and lunch." [Listen as he recites the problems he encountered as a result of forgetting his backpack and lunch.] "I can understand your frustration. That sounds hard. Let's make a plan so this doesn't happen again. What are your ideas?"

After a better way of organizing is in place, if your child still has a forgetful day, don't give up in frustration. Remember, we *all* have forgetful days. Give your child an encouraging hug and say, "I forget sometimes, too. You're making an effort and making progress! I know that tomorrow will be a better day."

For the child who is continually disobedient—and explains it away with "I just forgot"—you can say, "Forgetting for you is a choice. You can choose to remember and do what you know is right. Saying 'I forgot'—when you simply chose to ignore instructions—is a lie. I won't accept that.

"If you continue to choose not to take your backpack, you'll be hungry at lunch and you won't have the things you need for school. If you choose to let your grades drop because you don't turn in homework, along with that choice comes cutbacks on after-school fun and you may need to attend summer school.

"Honey, I believe you can change your behavior. I want you to enjoy the rewards of happy lunchtimes with your friends, better grades, and self-respect. I'll be praying you make the best choice."

Wisdom from God's Word

The psalmist writes, "Are your wonders known in the darkness, or your righteousness in the land of forgetfulness? But I, O LORD, cry to you; in the morning my prayer comes before you" (Ps. 88:12–13).

Throughout Scripture, God instructs his children to *remember*—everything from important lessons on God's character to their identity as chosen people—and much more. At times, we see the children of Israel erecting monuments and markers to help ensure they don't forget (see 1 Sam. 7:12 for one example). Clearly, remembering is important to God.

See these related chapters:
Chapter 22: "Homework Hassles," page 143
Chapter 24: "Lying," page 152
Chapter 31: "Procrastination," page 191

20

Gossip and Tattling

You're driving your daughter, Sophie, and three friends to a dog park. The girls have been talking and giggling and it seems like innocent fun . . . until you hear several names mentioned.

Turning down the radio, you tune in to their conversation. What you overhear makes your heart heavy. The girls are gossiping. And each time the conversation lulls, Sophie seems to delight in reviving it with a fresh flurry of mean-spirited comments. Clearly, the backseat belly laughs are coming at the expense of others.

How could your daughter think this is okay? It's time for some boundary-making . . . and heart-shaping.

What Is the Difference between Gossip and Tattling?

Gossip involves sharing unflattering, private, scandalous, or distorted information between peers. Tattling is the unsolicited reporting—to an adult, teacher, parent, or other authority figure—of another child's perceived wrongdoing.

Typically, tattling begins during the preschool years. Gossip, however, is more likely to begin when children are school-age, as their verbal skills advance and kids become more attuned to peer influence. Though more often connected with girls because of their verbal nature, kids of *both* genders tattle and gossip.

With tattling, it is important to discern the difference between "sharing information" in a helpful way for the purpose of righting a wrong (preventing a danger, etc.) versus reporting on other children's activities to get them in trouble. Unaddressed, tattling can alienate a child from siblings and peers. Gossip, when ignored by parents, teachers, and others, can become a brutal weapon wielded by bullies (see chap. 10 "Bullying" on p. 79) and cliquish children (see chap. 15 "Cliques" on p. 106), causing untold emotional damage.

What Could You Do?

Tattling

- If your child is a tattler, search for her emotional payoff. Is she seeking love? Security? Significance? Or a combination of all three? (See p. 21.) If so, help her meet these legitimate needs in legitimate ways.
- Help your child understand how tattling differs from beneficial types of communication. To draw the distinction, focus on *motives* and the condition of the heart.
- Encourage your child to tell you when someone is doing something that will hurt her or someone else.
  - For example, this means *always* telling you when someone, even a family member, tries to touch your child or another child in a place covered by a bathing suit. (See chap. 33 "Sexual Curiosity" on p. 200 and chap. 34 "Sexual Storms" on p. 204.)
  - Provide other examples to help your child understand definitions and boundaries.

Gossiping

- Teach your child what gossip is, using simple terms that relate to her age.
- Set an example by not gossiping.
- Ask God to help you identify your child's motive for gossiping. Does it make her feel superior to others? Does she hope to cement a bond with those in her group? Does she crave attention?

- Clearly communicate that gossiping is unacceptable and explain why. Over the following days and weeks, review Scriptures on gossip and the tongue: Proverbs 13:3; 16:28; 26:20–22; Psalms 17:3; 39:1; 141:3; Ephesians 4:29; 2 Timothy 2:16; and 1 Peter 2:1. Together with your daughter, choose several verses to memorize.
- In addition to telling her what *not* to do (gossip), teach your child what *to* do. For example:
  - Focus on the best in others (Eph. 4:32).
  - Examine her heart before attempting to solve a problem (Matt. 7:3–5).
  - Check her motives before talking about others (1 Thess. 2:4).
  - Speak sensitively, honestly, and lovingly (Col. 4:6).
  - Make resolution and reconciliation her heart's desire (Matthew 18).
- With your child, role-play ways to handle real-life situations where others gossip in her presence.
- For a child who gossips in writing (by text message or e-mail, for example), read one of her messages back to her. Ask how she would feel if someone communicated the same things about her. (See chap. 26 "Media Mania" on p. 164.)
- As a family, pledge to stop using critical and complaining words.

In the case of your daughter, who was gossiping with friends on the way to the dog park, you could also:

- Pray with her about her actions.
- Ground her until she provides you with a plan for apologizing to the girls *about whom* she was gossiping and makes arrangements to ask for their forgiveness. It's likely you'll need to coach your child through creating the plan. Ensure it includes ways to:
  - Correct any false information your daughter may have passed along.
  - Get to know the girls about whom she was gossiping, if possible.

- Consider whether God may be calling you and your daughter to positively impact the lives of these girls. (See chap. 15 "Cliques" on p. 106.)
- Ensure she apologizes and asks forgiveness from the girls *with whom* she was gossiping. Be certain she apologizes for her poor behavior and influence and shares with them her new resolve not to gossip about people but, instead, to reach out to them with an open heart.

What Could You Say?

After you bring the girls home from the park, you could talk to them together and say, "You girls are such good friends. I can see how much you enjoy talking, laughing, and having fun together. And that's wonderful.

"On the way to the dog park this morning, I heard some things that concern me . . . and I'd like your thoughts. Do you know what gossip is?" [Listen carefully to their replies.] "It's talking about others in a way that judges, criticizes, or hurts their reputation. It is an easy habit to get into, but it's a bad habit to have."

Next, give each child an attractive "gift bag" filled with something that smells *terrible* (old garbage or strong-smelling cheese, for instance). After they open their bags, say, "It stinks, doesn't it? Would any of you like to have more? If I gave you a gift bag for your birthday—filled with smelly garbage—how would you feel?" [Allow the children time to reply to each question.] "When I take these bags to the garbage can, notice how the smell stays behind." [Discard the bags.]

"Gossip is the same way. It's like smelly garbage coming from your heart and out of your mouth. It not only hurts the person you're talking about, but it hurts you, too. The Bible says, 'There is nothing outside a person that by going into him can defile him, but the things that come out of a person are what defile him' (Mark 7:15). Gossip makes your heart unclean. And it makes God's heart sad."

Next, give each child a gift bag with something fragrant inside (a freshly cut orange, a fabric softener sheet—anything your child would enjoy smelling). "The Bible says that through us, Jesus 'spreads the fragrance of the knowledge of him everywhere'" (2 Cor. 2:14).

As you discuss the meaning of this verse, you could say, "People know the kind of person you are by what you say and do. Use your words to encourage and build others up. That way, even after you leave, the memory of the good things you've said stays behind—just like a wonderful smell.[1]

"One of the biggest choices you make as you grow up is what words you use. You control what you say. If you're with people who gossip, change the subject. If they keep gossiping, *leave*. If you can't leave, don't join in. Instead, choose to be quiet for a while and pray silently or think about Scripture. This lets you practice being the kind of person God created you to be.

"You need to decide now what kind of smell you're going to leave behind as you go through life—foul or sweet? My prayer is that from now on you'll choose to stop gossiping and begin leaving behind a sweet smell that will honor God and you that will bless others."

Later, after her friends leave, you could ask your child, "What do you think about gossip now?" [Wait and listen.] "I need you to know that if you choose to gossip, you'll be choosing not to spend time with friends who gossip with you. You'll also be choosing for me to be with you when you're with *any* friends, so I can listen to what you say. That's not what I want, and I know it's not what you want either. But this is very important, and if you need help controlling your words . . . I want to help you.

"In the meantime, you're to stay home and not communicate with your friends until you can tell me how you plan to ask forgiveness from the people you've gossiped about and how you'll correct the wrong things you said to the girls you were gossiping with. I'm especially interested to hear how you're going to use words to build people up—leaving behind a sweet fragrance.

"I love you and you're very precious to me—and to God. I know you can find ways to use your words for good. And I want you always to remember: I'm here to help you!"

Wisdom from God's Word

The Bible is clear about the incredible power of the tongue for good or evil. "A gentle tongue is a tree of life, but perverseness in it breaks the spirit" (Prov. 15:4). We have all been hurt by someone's careless and unkind words. That experience can serve to remind us and our children to use words that encourage, not discourage. Hebrews 3:13 says it best: "Encourage one another daily."

See these related chapters:

21

Harmful Habits and Addictions

During a regular checkup, the dentist of your eleven-year-old daughter suggests you schedule a series of return visits to have her cavities filled. "The number of problems throughout Cammie's teeth tells me something has significantly changed in her diet since last year," the dentist announces. "She needs to cut way back on sweets—especially the sugary sodas. Drinking those all day will guarantee a mouthful of decay."

All day? You assure the dentist your family only serves sugary drinks on special occasions. *So you wonder, where could all that sugar be coming from?*

Back home, you discover all kinds of candy hidden in Cammie's bedroom drawers with wads of wrappers stashed under the bed. A phone call to her teacher confirms that your daughter often arrives at school finishing off cola and candy.

You realize this is more than a sweet tooth. She may have a sugar addiction.

What Is Addiction?

In simple terms, children are addicted when they become preoccupied with a substance or an activity to the degree that they neglect their vital relationships, their responsibilities, and then they compromise their integrity. Addicted children feel they can never get enough to be satisfied. This drives their increasing pull toward addiction and the need to cleverly cover their tracks.

Many children may dedicate much attention to their interests—without developing addictions. But when an interest supersedes their important activities and relationships—when it becomes more important than anything else—it has crossed into the realm of addiction.

Foods that spike blood sugar have been shown to be biologically addictive.[1] Addictions to sugar and caffeine are becoming increasingly common in children, as well as addictions to video games, the Internet, and other media.[2]

Signs of addiction to video games include:[3]

- Distress, frustration, or irritability when they cannot play.
- An inability to turn their attention to other priorities.
- Game time is completely out of proportion to time spent interacting with family and friends.
- Loss of interest in once-pleasurable activities.
- Falling behind in school and failing grades.
- Lying about completing homework or receiving finishing tasks to spend more time playing games.

Addictive patterns can encroach into a child's life subtly. Addictions may also reflect the harmful habits that many parents may not be ready to see or admit in themselves. Has chronic overeating become your comfort? To relax, must you drink alcohol each day? Do you choose medication as the first solution for every emotional and physical discomfort? Even exercise can become an addiction when carried to an extreme.

Harmful habits can serve as a way to self-medicate when feeling out of control or insecure. In these cases, efforts to stop the objectionable *behavior*—apart from addressing the underlying cause—could prompt your child to abandon one addiction only to be ensnared by another. Your job, therefore, is to help your child identify and heal any *underlying pain* that may be fueling an addiction.

What Could You Do?

How you handle your child's addiction depends on her age and the nature of the addiction. For example:

- If you suspect an addiction, meet first with your family doctor to rule out any underlying physical issues such as diabetes, thyroid problems, a vitamin deficiency, or chemical imbalance.
- Talk with your child about any involvement with the substance or activity that concerns you.
  - Show her any physical evidence of addiction.
  - Ask her to tell you her thoughts and what's going on physically in her body. Listen without interrupting.
  - Your child may not be able to verbalize what is driving her addictions. Either way, assure her that both you and God love her unconditionally and will do whatever is best for her.
- Explain how addictions work and how they are curable.
- If your daughter is addicted, assemble a team of experts to develop an individualized plan—one that includes developing new skills, increasing self-worth, ending the addiction, and making healthy choices. For example, the team may include your child's doctor, teacher, school nurse, day care provider, and a trained therapist.
- Tell your child the two of you will be getting expert help to learn how to overcome the cravings. Give the strong assurance that you'll work together as a team, with God as the Captain.
- Meet with a therapist who can help your child address emotional factors that may be driving this harmful habit. For instance, has divorce, death, remarriage, or relocation caused any emotional upheaval? Is your child being bullied . . . or abused?
- For children under the age of seven, you may wish to completely remove the offending substance or activity from the child's environment. For school-age children, a slow weaning may be best. In either case, expect resistance. The addiction is meeting a need in your child that should be fulfilled through healthy means—a legitimate need that must not be ignored.

- Brainstorm with your child about solutions. Ask, "Do you have any ideas you think will help?"
- Realize, this is an opportunity to strengthen your child's ability to make wise choices even when feeling insecure or hurt. Resist the temptation to shift into "control overdrive," which demotivates children from exercising self-discipline—driving them back into secrecy.
- Consider helping your child take on responsibility—such as caring for a neighbor's pet, doing community volunteer work, or raking leaves. Being active, productive, and accountable nurtures a sense of worth and self-control.
- Enroll your child in group sports or in music, dance, or drawing lessons—activities that foster self-discipline, feelings of accomplishment, and new relationships.
- Camps and counseling centers created specifically to wean and rehabilitate children addicted to the Internet and other media are a growing phenomenon in many countries and are springing up worldwide.[4] Likewise, weight loss camps, once an adult's domain, are now available for children.[5]
- Without smothering or hovering, you might need to spend more time with your child during this recovery period.
- Assess the family schedule. If you are stressed, overwhelmed, or too busy, then adjust and make your home a place of peace and security.

What Could You Say?

In the case of your daughter who struggles with a sugar addiction, you could say, "Honey, your dentist said you need to cut way back on sugar. I realize this won't be easy. But if you and I and the Lord work together as a team, we can do it.

"I also know you've been hiding the amount of sweets you're eating and drinking. I found these candy wrappers in your bedroom [show them], and I know you've been drinking sodas before school.

"When something becomes so important to you that you feel you have to hide it and you're willing to sneak around to get it, you've made it more important than your honesty and integrity. Integrity is doing what's right even when no one but God is looking. All of that means you are probably addicted to it.

"I know it doesn't feel good to keep something important in your life secret—and to crave something you're not allowed to have. We're going to meet with our family doctor to see if this sugar craving is coming from an unmet need in your body. We're also going to talk with a therapist to see how we can help you feel secure and satisfied—without the sugar.

"To help you make good choices, I'm taking the junk food out of our home. We're going grocery shopping and, together, we'll pick out cereal, drinks, and snacks that taste good but that are better for you. For the next few weeks, each day after school we're going to talk about how you are feeling and what you ate and drank that day.

"If you keep buying sodas and sweets, you will forfeit your allowance. If you are getting sweets without buying them, we will limit your activities for a time to places where sweets aren't available.

"Getting involved in an activity that interests you will also be helpful. Here's a list of options. I'd like your thoughts on which one(s) you'd enjoy the most.

"We're going to work on this as a team and develop a plan to wean you away from sugar. I know you can do this, and I'm here to help you every step of the way . . . and God is too. He promises that 'he will not let you be tempted beyond your ability, but with the temptation he will also provide the way of escape, that you may be able to endure it' (1 Cor. 10:13).

"By your next dental checkup, I'm expecting your number of cavities to be cut in half. When that happens, we're going to celebrate with a camping trip."

Wisdom from God's Word

When your daughter is pressured to make wrong choices, teach her to bring her habits and temptations to the Lord, claiming this powerful promise: "We are more than conquerors through him who loved us" (Rom. 8:37).

See these related chapters:
Chapter 25: "Mealtime Tussles," page 158
Chapter 26: "Media Mania," page 164
Chapter 38: "Substance Abuse," page 223

22

Homework Hassles

"It's too hard." . . . "It's boring." . . . "Why do I have to learn this?" . . . "I already know this stuff."

Your daughter, Nicole, won't do her homework unless you insist, and then she drags it out. Half the time she forgets to turn it in . . . even after it's finished.

These assignments are important to her grades. But how much can she learn when each homework session involves more complaining than completing the work?

What Could You Do?

Help your child discover her individual style of learning. Then structure a homework regimen to complement her style. Though more sophisticated assessments are available, here are three quick and easy ways to think about the learning styles:

Auditory learners learn best from hearing the information they need to retain. Read instructions aloud and use a voice recorder so they can play back key points to increase retention.

Visual learners retain information best when lessons are accompanied by illustrations and other visual aids. Give your visual learners a notebook and bright pens or pencils to take notes or draw pictures of key concepts as they work.

Kinesthetic learners learn best from a hands-on approach and physical activity (even more than the average child). Let kinesthetic learners sit on an exercise ball while doing homework . . . or act out a dramatic presentation of what they are learning . . . or artistically draw out scenes (from history lessons).[1]

Don't confuse your own preferred way to learn as being the *only* way . . . or the *best* way. What's best is what works for *your* child. Your role is to equip, encourage, and empower your daughter. Consider incorporating these elements into her homework routine:

- Designate a time and place to do homework and be available to offer help when needed. If your child can't work independently, sitting near you may help until she matures. This will also help you monitor her progress unobtrusively. (You want her to see you as a support, not a critic or crutch.)
- Don't permit your child to multitask when working on homework (no watching TV, playing video games, texting, etc.). Multitasking is a myth. In reality, a child's brain cannot assimilate information properly while engaged in multiple tasks.
- Teach your child to break large assignments into manageable pieces and tackle distasteful tasks first, then afterward, be rewarded by doing the fun, easy parts.
- Have your child write "Homework to Turn In" on a clear plastic folder and put it in the front of her binder. With a smile in your voice, say, "Any time you open your binder and see papers in that folder, a little bell should go off in your brain and keep ringing until you turn in your homework!"
- Check homework as soon as it's completed so that any needed change can be done well before bedtime.
- Some children study best in total silence. Others find that instrumental music helps them focus. Determine what works best for your child.
- Take into consideration your child's strengths. For one who naturally excels in science but struggles in math, it may be necessary to accept passing grades in a more difficult subject (assuming she's giving her best effort). Success in areas of strength often motivates performance in weaker areas as well. More

than likely she will later in life anchor her career in an area of natural ability.

- Children can *appear* busy for long periods without making progress. Be aware of what's actually being accomplished versus the amount of time your child spends looking busy.
  - Give your child ten- to fifteen-minute breaks, as needed.
  - Clearly define what activities are acceptable during the breaks. For instance, permit your child to eat a snack, engage in a physical activity, or play a short nonelectronic game.
- Create a special reward for cultivating good homework habits. For example, at the end of each week that homework is completed, she could select a reward from a basket stocked with fun, inexpensive items you know she'll enjoy. Or encourage her to drop a dozen beans into a jar each day she does homework without hassles. After a month of putting beans in the "homework jar," make bean soup together and celebrate with a special outing. (See chap. 4 "Your R & R Toolkit" on p. 38 for more ideas.)
- As tempting as it may be, don't do your child's homework. She's the student, not you.
- Consider using a tutor to help her master difficult subjects.
- If homework is a problem and grades are dropping, your child may need to be screened for a learning *difference* (e.g., dyslexia) or require specialized training to learn how to study.
- Give a short-term repercussion for *choosing* to stray off task. Not being able to play with a favorite toy or game or not being allowed to attend a fun activity may be enough to trigger improvement.
- A *long-term repercussion* is appropriate when grades fall below a predetermined standard.
  - Realistically assess your child's abilities. Do you need to cut back on extracurricular activities that overshadow academics? Only take away something helpful to your child's development (ballet or band) *if* academics can't be improved through other means.

- Experiencing a natural consequence, such as being dropped from a team for substandard grades, may be the very best teacher.

What Could You Say?

In the case of your daughter, who complains, procrastinates, and makes excuses, you could say, "Honey, I believe in you and your ability to learn. Learning prepares you for the rest of your life.

"Homework is a huge part of learning. When you choose to keep up with your homework, your reward will be more freedom. Another reward will be the fun of learning and feeling good about yourself. Once your homework's done, you'll have time for other things you like to do.

"If you choose not to do your homework, you'll also be choosing not to play or watch television or use video games and the computer for a while.

"I work each day and so do you. School is your job. Playtime doesn't start until your schoolwork is done. After school, you'll sit near me until your homework is done and until I hear from your teacher that she's receiving it each day on time.

"I'm going to ask you questions that will help me know how to best arrange your homework area." [For each question, ask what your child thinks, then share your observations. If your child is too young to know, skip this exercise. You decide based on your own observations.]

- Do you learn better when people are around or when you are alone?
- Do you prefer to study at the kitchen table, in the den when the family is not around, or alone in your room?
- Does it help when I quiz you before a test?
- Do you remember more when you *see* what you're studying or when you *talk* about it?
- Does it help you to move around when you study?

When your child completes her homework successfully, emphasize her *effort* (not just her ability) by saying, "I'm proud of how hard you worked on that!"

Wisdom from God's Word

God fashioned us uniquely and helps us use our various learning styles by presenting truth in a variety of ways—from parables, psalms, and illustrations to analogies and activities. And to help us further understand, Christ came to teach by example. Then he sent the Holy Spirit to be our Conscience, Counselor, and Comforter. So when you provide customized ways to learn, your child's homework and learning can become positive experiences.

"Whoever heeds instruction is on the path of life, but he who regrets reproof leads others astray" (Prov. 10:17).

See Chapter 31: "Procrastination," page 191

23

Interrupting

You and your daughter, Madison, are having a much-anticipated lunch date with dear friends and their children. It's a pleasant afternoon—with a single exception. As you recount a fun family event, Madison interrupts.

"Tell them about what happened before that."

You begin again.

"No, it wasn't *that* day," she butts in. "It was the day before."

Embarrassed, you give her a look that says, "Stop interrupting and let *me* tell this story!"

A minute later, as a friend shares a similar experience, Madison interrupts again, inserting trivial details and turning the conversation back to herself.

You don't want to dampen your daughter's delight for expression, but how can you help her stop interrupting and become a respectful communicator?

Why Is It Important to Cultivate Delayed Gratification in Childhood?

When your child learns to wait her turn to speak, she's learning delayed gratification, patience, and other traits that will benefit her for a lifetime. A scientific experiment known as the Marshmallow Test illustrates this point.

Researchers set a marshmallow on a plate in a room occupied by one child after another. An adult told the children they could eat the marshmallow right away, or if they waited until the adult returned, they could have *two* marshmallows. Some children avoided temptation by turning their backs to the marshmallow. Others covered their faces, only to peek through their fingers at the marshmallow. Using the tip of the tongue, a few took tiny tastes. Still others ate the marshmallow the minute the adult was out of the room. Researchers who followed the children for decades as they matured found that the same subjects who controlled their desire to eat the marshmallow instantly were better adjusted and more successful as teens and adults.[1]

What Could You Do?

- While she is young, begin modeling and teaching respectful, effective communication skills.
- Even as she begins to speak, teach her to wait her turn and not monopolize the conversation. Constantly yielding the floor to a child's every whim fosters impatience and more interruptions.
- If she wants to ask or say something important when you're talking, teach your child to place her hand subtly on your shoulder (if you're seated) or your arm or leg (if you're standing) and then wait to be invited to speak. (Emergencies are, of course, the exception.)
- Don't rush conversation for fear that your child will interrupt if she has to wait for more than a few seconds. Children have an amazing ability to adapt to the boundaries you enforce. Impatience results when your boundaries are nonexistent or inconsistent.
- Acknowledge your child's turn to speak at an appropriate break in the conversation.
- As your child matures, teach her to use conversation starters— questions that draw people out and help her get to know them.
- Ask your child to consider what *silent* and *listen* have in common. If she doesn't notice, point out that each word contains identical letters.

The Bible says, "Everyone should be quick to listen, slow to speak, and slow to become angry" (James 1:19 NIV).

What Could You Say?

In the case of your daughter, who repeatedly interrupted at lunch, you could say, "I know you were excited to go out with friends today. I was too. Tell me: What did you learn about the other children who were with us at lunch?" [Listen.] "What happened when the others told a story? What happened when I was talking?" [Listen to her reply and check for recognition of your point.]

"Honey, you chose to do most of the talking and nearly all of the interrupting at lunch. I truly believe you didn't do this to hurt anyone's feelings or to show disrespect. But that's what happens when you constantly interrupt people who are talking. How would you feel if other people didn't let you finish telling your stories and cut in often to correct little details?" [Let her reply.]

Use a ball to demonstrate how polite conversation works. Say, "Conversation is like a game where one player asks a question." [Toss the ball to her.] "Now you respond with comments and a question. That returns the conversation back to me." [Hold out your hands as she tosses the ball back to you.] "Now it's my turn to speak." [Throw the ball back to your child.] "Then it's your turn to speak." [Practice a back-and-forth conversation while tossing the ball.]

Next say, "I want to help you break the habit of interrupting so you can become a good listener, which will help make you a good friend. This is something I, too, had to learn when I was growing up. It's not a skill we're born with. These three rules will help you when others are talking:

"Number 1: Listen to others the same way you want them to listen to you—without interrupting. Jesus said, 'Whatever you wish that others would do to you, do also to them' (Matt. 7:12). That's called the Golden Rule.

"Number 2: Let people tell a story the way *they* want to tell it.

It's *their* story, not yours. If you think the story happened a little differently, you can tell me later when we're alone. Cutting in to correct a person about something small can be annoying. If the teller needs help remembering, she'll ask.

"Number 3: Remember it's okay for people to like and dislike different things. A movie you don't like may be somebody else's favorite. A person may like skateboarding while you enjoy biking. Allow others to have their own opinions. God made us unique, like snowflakes. No two are alike. That's God's design and we honor it when we accept that people have their own likes and dislikes."

Check for understanding of the rules, then continue. "If you choose to follow the rules when others are talking, I'll be eager to bring you along on fun outings like the one today. But if you choose not to follow the rules, you'll also be choosing not to come.

"The Bible says, 'Do nothing from rivalry or conceit, but in humility count others more significant than yourselves' (Phil. 2:3 ESVUK). Let's talk about what that means." [Do so.] "I want you to practice considering others and what they have to say as very important—even more important than what *you* have to say. As you do, you'll find that other people will want to talk to you and be your friend. I know that's what you want and, personally, I'm positive you have everything it takes to be a great listener!"

Wisdom from God's Word

Lovingly show a child who regularly interrupts that she can exchange self-focus for humility and lack of control for delayed gratification. "For by the grace given to me I say to everyone among you not to think of himself more highly than he ought to think, but to think with sober judgment, each according to the measure of faith that God has assigned" (Rom. 12:3).

Lying

Your daughter, Chloe, doesn't realize you can hear her conversation with a friend as they play in the backyard after school. But the open window carries their voices to the kitchen table where you sit mulling over monthly bills.

"I'm going on vacation to Disney World this summer," Chloe's friend announces proudly.

"So what? I've been there . . . three times," Chloe shoots back.

"No, you haven't!" her friend protests.

"Have too!" Chloe insists indignantly.

Chloe has never been to Disney World. You know that and so does she. So why . . . the lie?

Why Do Children Lie?

Lying is part of our fallen human condition (John 8:44). The only person who has never lied is Jesus.

Developmentally, preschoolers may not be able to discern the difference between truth and make-believe. Even five- and six-year-olds may still confuse the two sometimes until their grasp of truth and fiction matures.[1]

When older children lie intentionally, they may do so for many reasons, all of which are rooted in our inborn sinful nature (Rom. 3:23), which brings with it a tendency to:

- Mistrust God, who cannot lie (Titus 1:2);
- Deceive ourselves—to hide from the truth (Ps. 51:5);
- Envy others (Gen. 30:1);
- Desire to harm others (1 Sam. 18:9; 19:1);
- Profit personally (Gen. 27:21–24).

In addition, children may lie to:

- Look good before others (Luke 18:11);
- Receive praise and recognition (John 12:43);
- Escape negative consequences (Neh. 9:33);
- Avoid being exposed (Prov. 12:13);
- Avoid conflict (Isa. 28:15).

Children who lie rarely perceive themselves as liars. Instead, they're trying to get their needs met illegitimately. If a pattern of lying persists, look for the deeper root cause(s), primarily:

- Feeling *insignificant* and lying to appear more important
- Feeling *insecure* and lying to avoid looking bad, stupid, or in-adequate

When our God-given inner needs for significance and security are not met, especially in childhood, the tendency is to try to fill those needs in other ways.[2]

Are Some Lies Harmless?

No, not in God's economy. Over time, repeated lying deadens the conscience—making it easier and easier to be deceptive. So what, exactly, does it mean to lie?

- *Lies* are untrue statements told with the intent to deceive (Prov. 14:5).
- *Half-truths* are partially true statements made with the delib-erate intent to deceive. They contain just enough truth to be convincing (Gen. 12:13).

- *Deception* is intentionally giving a false impression whether through a statement or by omission (Ps. 12:2). Deception may be verbal, written, or conveyed through body language.
- *White lies* are untrue statements that appear harmless and unimportant, but they are still deliberate lies (Heb. 3:13).[3]

Covering a lie often requires spinning a web of additional untruths—ongoing sin that distances your child from God and others. Instead, the Bible says, "Stop telling lies. Let us tell our neighbors the truth, for we are all parts of the same body" (Eph. 4:25 NLT).

What Could You Do?

Proverbs 6:17 states that the Lord detests a "lying tongue." Lying is not cute, nor is it a behavior your child will outgrow without adult intervention. Therefore, it's important to:

- Consider your home environment.
  - If a parent is harsh or unpredictable, a child may lie to avoid outbursts. Make your home a safe and nurturing place with consistent, fair boundaries.
  - Set an example of telling the truth in your own life, even if (or especially when) a lie might be more convenient.
- Show your child she is loved, significant, and secure—and help her understand her God-given worth as a context for correction and training in righteousness.
- If there's doubt, clarify *what is truth* and *what are lies* to help your child know the difference and choose wisely.
- Require that your child seek forgiveness when she lies to you or someone else.
- As she matures, help her understand what it means to "speak the truth in love" (Eph. 4:15) and to exercise discretion. Being truthful doesn't always mean telling everyone everything in a tactless way.
- Extend mercy if your child does something wrong and, rather than concealing her sin by lying, she voluntarily confesses it with sincere repentance.[4]

- Together, watch the movie *Pinocchio* or read the book. Then talk about the repercussions of lying. Why did Pinocchio lie? What was the result? What could Pinocchio and your child do differently? In addition, read the story of *The Boy Who Cried Wolf*. Discuss how lies affect others and cause them to distrust—even when the truth is told.
- Assure your child that she can *decide* to tell the truth, beginning immediately. When you "catch" her doing so—especially when lying would have better served her personal interests—praise her character and let her know how proud you are of her godly choice.
- If lying has become habitual, diligently work with your child until she breaks the habit.
- Together, memorize Psalm 141:3: "Set a guard, O LORD, over my mouth; keep watch over the door of my lips!"

In the case of your daughter, who lied to her friend about going to Disney World, you could also:

- Draw out your child to get to the heart of *why* she lied, helping her address the root cause. For example, was she feeling envious that she had never been to Disney World? Without excusing the lie, help her communicate her true feelings in a safe and supportive manner.
- Share biblical principles to guide her to understand God's heart on the matter.
- Accompany your daughter to tell her friend that she lied and to apologize.

What Could You Say?

In the case of your daughter, who lied about visiting Disney World, you could say:

"When you say something you know isn't true, you're telling a lie. I expect you to tell me the complete truth—not leaving out something I need to know, even if I don't ask. And I also expect nothing but the truth.[5]

"That's what God wants, too. The Bible says, 'People who conceal their sins will not prosper, but if they confess and turn from them, they will receive mercy' (Prov. 28:13 NLT). *Mercy* means they won't get what they deserve for doing something wrong."

Next, place a wooden ruler on top of two cups to form a bridge so that the cups are as far apart as possible yet still support the "bridge" ruler. Explain to your daughter that the ruler is a symbol of "trust" between each of you, represented by the two cups. Ask her to tell you what the word *trust* means and briefly amplify if needed.

Now, take the ruler and break it in two pieces. Try to place the broken pieces back on the cups where they were before. Show her that the pieces won't balance as they did before and now a gap is left. Leave the cups separated and balance one piece of the ruler on each cup explaining, "When trust is broken, the bridge that connects us breaks too. And now there's a gap in our relationship."

Then, move the cups closer together so the pieces of the ruler again touch. "See how even though we can draw closer to try to rebuild our bridge of trust, there is still brokenness and a gap. What do we need to use to fix the gap?" If your daughter doesn't immediately suggest it, bring out the glue . . . but not an instant bonding variety. Use good, old-fashioned school glue. "Rebuilding our trust bridge will take time, just like the glue needs time to set.

"Can you put the ruler back together exactly as it was? [Wait for her *no*.] That's how it is with trust. It's very precious and must be handled with care. When we break trust, we can't undo it. What we *can* do is rebuild trust. But that takes time and effort.

"Sweetheart, I will always love you, *no matter what*! But there are things you can do to lose my trust. Lying is one of them. When trust is broken, you won't get it back easily, not because I won't forgive you, but because it takes time to rebuild.

"When you lie, you're telling me I need to question everything you say, watch everything you do, and check everything you tell me. I will say *no* to more of your requests—not to punish you, but because you've chosen to break our trust.

"When you choose to be honest, it shows me you're ready to make more choices about the things that are important to you and that you can be trusted with more freedom."

Now, add a third cup to support the broken part of the ruler that's been glued and say, "God is able to restore our relationship after trust is broken. And he can do such a good job you'd never even know it was broken! But for that to happen, you need to stop lying and start telling the truth, even when you think a lie would serve you better. He will be the support that gets us through this.

"I want you to enjoy the blessings of God that come with being truthful—and the peace that comes with not hiding wrong things you've done. The Bible talks about the joys of a clean conscience (1 Pet. 3:16). I know you've felt that joy many times before. Let's pray and ask God to help you find it again. He wants that for you, and so do I."

Wisdom from God's Word

When people speak to us, we all would like to believe that the words are 100 percent true. We all hate when people lie to us. How much more important that every word we speak be absolutely truthful. This verse from the book of Proverbs should give us the motivation to be a 100 percent truth teller: "Truthful words stand the test of time, but lies are soon exposed" (Prov. 12:19 NLT).

See these related chapters:
Chapter 13: "Cheating," page 95
Chapter 37: "Stealing," page 220

25

Mealtime Tussles

You planned for this all day: a hot, homemade dinner with family gathered around the table, lingering over meaningful moments, connecting, and making memories.

But someone flipped the script.

Slouched in his chair, Nicholas begins texting. Under the table, Beth kicks Josh, who is sneaking his vegetables to the dog. Finally, big sister Ellie walks in after turning on the TV in the den to keep an eye on her favorite reality show while eating.

Within moments, Beth's friend arrives to work on their science project, and everyone takes the newest distraction as their cue to scatter. Busy hands carry plates off to other rooms, and family time falls apart . . . *again*!

What Could You Do?

Family mealtimes are meant to nourish the souls as well as the bodies of your loved ones. Eating together supports healthy child development and lessens the likelihood of children engaging in "risky behaviors." Frequent meals together also improve school performance, family communication, and a child's overall contentment with life.[1]

Another compelling reason to share regular, nutritious mealtimes is that fast-food meals frequently are higher in calories, saturated fat, and sodium than ones prepared at home.[2] As childhood obesity rates continue to climb, nutritional awareness has never been more important.[3]

The following guidelines and boundaries can help you experience inviting mealtimes:

- Establish a precedent for shared mealtimes when your child is young.
- Set a regular, realistic time for family meals. While other obligations can't always be avoided, limit these to allow for at least three uninterrupted family meals per week. Invite your child to help choose a recipe. Encourage him to assist with the cooking. Creating meals together is a privilege, not a punishment.
- Use a special-recognition plate to commemorate family birthdays or significant accomplishments. Occasionally, use your best dishes for your favorite people—your family.
- Make a rule that *all* family members—adults and children—leave digital devices in another room. Barring an emergency, nothing is to interrupt a shared meal.
- Praise your child for arriving promptly for meals and for using good table manners.
- Keep mealtimes enjoyable. Initiate engaging, inclusive conversation, drawing your child in. Being involved in adult communication is a fundamental way children learn to master language. Laugh together. Share stories.
- Practice good manners—everyone at the table matters and deserves respect. This includes placing napkins on laps, using utensils properly, keeping hands and feet to yourself, chewing with your mouth closed, not talking with a mouthful of food, and listening to others without interrupting.
- Learn about each other's day, how your child is feeling, and what problems he's facing. Ask questions and listen "between the lines." Discuss spiritual matters, church involvement, and what God is doing in each family member's life.
- Fill a jar with conversation starters. When you "catch" your child using good mealtime manners, let him draw slips of paper

with questions such as: What made you laugh today? Where would you like to go on vacation? Who's your hero?

- Make it clear that poor attitudes are not to accompany your child to the table. If he has a poor attitude (assuming you've ruled out any serious underlying causes), give him a reasonable amount of time to correct it. If he doesn't, the repercussion could be a missed meal. Allow him to have a nutritious, nonsugary snack before bedtime if dinner is skipped.
- Use mealtimes to creatively engage your child's interest, participation, and imagination in spiritual pursuits. Reading Scripture, discussing memory verses, and praying together can bond family members to one another and to Christ. Deuteronomy 6:6–7 says, "And these words that I command you today shall be on your heart. You shall teach them diligently to your children, and shall talk of them when you sit in your house, and when you walk by the way, and when you lie down, and when you rise."
- Thank those who prepared the meal and/or served it.
- Teach your child appropriate behavior—not to scream, whine, complain, or run while inside restaurants. Remind him ahead of time to stay seated, eat quietly, be mindful of restaurant guests, and be polite to servers.

What's for Dinner?

The food you serve your child is vitally important to good health and behavior and to top performance academically and athletically. To impart healthy eating habits at home:

- Train your baby's taste buds to appreciate the flavors of less-sweet foods before being introduced to the sweetness of fruit. How? Consider introducing vegetables, grains, and beans, and then fruit—in that order.
- Teach your child to eat because he's *hungry*, not because he's *upset*. Emotional eating patterns can be hard to unlearn.
- Balance meals with quality sources of fat, carbohydrates, and protein. Include a variety of vegetables and fruits.

- Determine that your child will *sample* new food items before deciding he doesn't like them.
- Allow your child to pass on foods he truly doesn't like by politely saying, "No, thank you." There's no need for dramatic facial expressions and snide remarks.
- Remember, you're a parent, not a short-order cook. Occasionally you may wish to ask your child what he'd like to eat at mealtime. But in general, the parent should determine the menu. When you do ask for input, let your child choose from a few preselected healthy choices.
- Don't insist that a child finish eating everything on his plate. If he refuses to eat the meal you've prepared, refrigerate it and present it again for his next meal. Don't allow between-meal snacks in this instance.
- Set an example by drinking plenty of water and eating healthy portions of good foods.
- Serve your child water at each meal (in addition to another beverage if you wish, such as milk). Pack water bottles in lunches and to take on trips. Limit the supply of junk food in your home. Stock your pantry and refrigerator with fresh fruits and vegetables, nuts and seeds, hummus, peanut butter, yogurt, and other nutritious foods (adjusting for any known allergies). Keep fresh-cut vegetables and fruit on hand and encourage your child to reach for them as snacks. These practices will cultivate healthy food choices and good health overall. They will also decrease your child's potential to become addicted to sugars and additives that can impact learning and behavior.[4]
- Show your child how to read food labels and why it's vital to know what's in the food he's eating.
- Watch for signs of allergies as well as intolerance and sensitivities to food and additives, which can trigger misbehavior and learning difficulties.[5]
- Instruct your child how to select a balanced meal when eating away from home. Help him order from menus and oversee him at potlucks and parties until he's able to make consistently wise choices with portion size and selections.

- Reserve fast food, sodas, and sweets for rare occasions.
- Serve your child sweet cereal occasionally for dessert rather than for breakfast, when a sugar jolt can adversely affect blood sugar levels.[6] For the same reason, avoid serving sugary cereal before bedtime.

What Could You Say?

To communicate your expectations for family mealtimes, you could say, "Being with you at mealtimes is a highlight of my day. And I want it to be a highlight for you too. While it will take some adjustments, eating meals together will draw us closer as a family.

"I know there will be exceptions in our routines, but there will be at least [name a workable number] evening meals each week that we enjoy together." [For older children, you can say, "I expect you to plan activities with that in mind."]

"Whether we're eating at home or out, I expect you to use your best manners." [If you aren't sure your children know your specific expectations, review them now.]

"Nick and Ellie, there'll be no texting or television watching at the table. Ellie, please turn off the TV. Nick, please put your phone in your bedroom. Beth, feet are for walking and standing, not for kicking your brother. You need to apologize to Josh.

"Josh, I work hard to provide a balanced diet that will help you grow strong and healthy. Giving your vegetables to the dog is sneaky and wrong. It also wastes money and keeps you from getting the nutrition you need just like the dog needs to eat dog food that's nutritious for dogs.

"Here's another serving for you, Josh. In the future, if you choose to sneak food that you don't like to the dog, not only will you get an extra serving of that food but you will need to eat it before you get anything else.

"At our mealtimes, we'll share our favorite foods. We will also talk about what is going on in our lives—the best parts of our day and the hard times as well. We'll discuss, too, what God is showing us and what we are learning. Then we'll know how to pray for each other.

"I'm looking forward to fun family mealtimes together. There's no one I'd rather share, laugh, and pray with than *you!*"

Wisdom from God's Word

Shared mealtimes nurture relationships, build lifetime memories, and communicate value to each member of your family. Throughout the Gospels, you often see Jesus doing this with friends and followers (see Matt. 9:9–10; Mark 2:13–17; Luke 22:14–20; John 21:4–19). Shared meals were also central to early church life. "And day by day . . . breaking bread in their homes, they received their food with glad and generous hearts" (Acts 2:46). You can free your family from mealtime tussles by adhering to these words of instruction: "So, whether you eat or drink, or whatever you do, do all to the glory of God" (1 Cor. 10:31).

See these related chapters:
Chapter 21: "Harmful Habits and Addictions," page 137
Chapter 41: "Whining," page 238

Media Mania

An article you read left you apprehensive. The topic was children and technology, and it indicated that younger children watch more TV than teens.[1] Without cars or as many extracurricular activities as their older counterparts, children spend more time with media than they do with family, church, reading, and homework—*combined*!

You begin to wonder: *Is it wise for your eight-year-old son, Evan, to have a computer in his room?* While he's at school, you take a deep breath, turn on his computer, and follow your son's digital footprints. The time you spend sleuthing confirms that Evan is a digital junkie and that his online habits must change . . . *now*.

What Are the Risks of Misusing Media and Technology?

Expanding digital access can bring many blessings—including greater educational, social, and recreational opportunities for children. With increased access, however, comes an increased need to help your child make wise choices on what can be a dangerous online frontier.

Today's children may pack into their day eight to ten hours of media exposure.[2] A recent survey showed that nearly 75 percent of children eight years and under (and 40 percent of toddlers) had used a mobile device.[3]

Sleep problems among three- to five-year olds increase with each additional hour of daily media use, while online time in the evenings aggravates sleep problems even more. And while having a television in the bedroom increases the likelihood of sleep problems—probably due to more evening viewing—more than 40 percent of two- to four-year-olds have bedroom televisions.[4]

Children can become desensitized to real-life trauma through digital games that depict explicit violence and degradation to women, particularly when kids play these games to excess.[5] Addiction is another risk of unrestricted access.[6]

While playing nonviolent video (and other digital) games *in moderation* can boost hand-eye coordination and certain cognitive abilities, left unrestrained, technology can drain time and attention away from your child's important developmental activities. It also has become a favorite tool of sexual deviants and other criminals worldwide.

Finally, sexting (sending sexually explicit text messages) is a growing phenomenon among older children.[7] Researchers studying youth sexting concluded: "For young people, the primary technology-related threat is not 'stranger danger' . . . but technology-mediated sexual pressure from their peers."[8] The Bible gives this warning, "The integrity of the upright guides them, but the crookedness of the treacherous destroys them" (Prov. 11:3).

What Could You Do?

The American Academy of Pediatrics (AAP) discourages media use by children younger than two years old. If electronic media access is allowed, the AAP recommends extremely close parental oversight.[9]

- To help children over age three avoid excessive use of the Internet, social media, movies, television, and other technology, establish usage guidelines for each tool.
- Create online privacy settings for your child and share concrete "dos and don'ts" for safe, godly usage.
- Know the passwords to all your child's online accounts.

- Specify days, times, and places your child is permitted to use digital media.
  - Consider permitting access only on weekends or after schoolwork and chores have received full attention.
  - Balance the time your child spends staring at a screen with outdoor activities, board games, trips to the park, etc.
- Make a trade. For every hour your child invests in reading good books or practicing a constructive skill, he receives a weekend hour for a parent-approved digital activity.
- Regularly check your child's browser history and review the websites he visits. Inform him of age restrictions for the most popular social media sites. If he's interested in becoming active on kid-friendly sites, visit his social media pages and friend lists. Also, review texts, instant message history, e-mails, and voice messages.
- Be savvy about your child's digital world and get to know other parents who prioritize awareness.
- Invite your child to share technology with you. Kids like showing what they know. Be a part of their world.
- Be available to help your child determine if/how to respond to challenging or inappropriate digital interactions.
- If he *accidentally* stumbles upon dangerous territory (which is easy to do), don't scold him. Instead, help him make a quick exit and assure him that you're always available to help.
- Let him know that you have installed monitoring software to proactively block access to certain online locations and activities, protecting him from inappropriate discoveries and predators.
  - Another option is to install software that operates in the background, silently tracking and reporting your child's every online move (with or without your child's knowledge, depending on your individual preference).
- Set up the computer in a heavily trafficked area of the home such as the family room—not your child's bedroom. Restrict portable laptop and electronic tablet use to this area.
- If your child violates the rules, further restrict his online access to times when you are present (at least until he has regained your trust).

- Insist that schoolwork be completed before your child goes online recreationally.
- If spending time online detracts from grades and important relationships, "pull the plug" until positive changes are made. Model restrained technology use. Make time for face-to-face conversation with your child. Don't check your texts and e-mails at family meals. Turn off the television when you're not watching it. Let your children see you controlling your media, versus your media controlling you.[10]
- Limit your child's cell phone plan to phone calls and text messages only. You may also decide to limit the number of phone calls and texts made in a given day, week, or month. Limit the number of contacts your child keeps on his phone. And consider giving your child a phone that does not include a camera. (See chap. 12 "Cell Phone Struggles" on p. 89.)
- Study Scripture about the importance of moral purity (e.g., Ps. 101:3; Prov. 10:9; 11:3) and talk with your child about what type of content is permissible and what is not. Psalm 101:3 says, "I will refuse to look at anything vile and vulgar" (NLT).

Should your child be unwilling to abide by the digital boundaries you've set, let him know he is choosing for you to disconnect him from all devices until there's an attitude change and a *demonstration* of cooperation.

What Could You Say?

"Using computers and video games is a big part of your life. And that's good . . . as long as it helps you live a life that pleases God. There are many fun, interesting places to go online. But there are also many dangerous places too—traps set by bad people hoping to trick you into going where you don't mean to go.

"Today, I looked through the history on your web browser and I was concerned by what I saw. Spending three or four hours a day on your computer is not what's best for you.

"I'm moving your computer to the den and installing software to help keep everyone who uses it from accidentally going to harmful websites. I'll be watching your online activity, and someone even more important will be watching, too—Jesus. Your heart is Jesus's home. So wherever you go online, you take him with you. Proverbs 15:3 says, 'The eyes of the LORD are in every place, keeping watch on the evil and the good.' When you visit a website or play a video game, ask yourself, 'Is this something Jesus would want me to look at?'

"From now on, your time online will be limited to one hour a day, beginning after your homework and chores are complete. If they're not finished before [time], you will not have any online time that day. I know this may be hard for you at first, but we can work together to find fun and helpful ways to spend your extra time.

"In our home, there's a reward when you choose to use technology wisely: you get to keep using it! Over time, as I see your judgment improve, you'll earn even more freedom. But if you choose to misuse technology, you'll be choosing to have it taken away for a period of time.

"Together, we're going to memorize Philippians 4:8, which says, 'Whatever is true, whatever is honorable, whatever is just, whatever is pure, whatever is lovely, whatever is commendable, if there is any excellence, if there is anything worthy of praise, think about these things.' If something you're doing online doesn't fit this description, make a different choice. If you're not sure, come ask me. One of my favorite parts about being your parent is helping you learn to make good choices.

"You've been entrusted with the privilege of using the Internet and other tools to connect to people and information. I feel sure you can use this privilege in a way that honors God."

Wisdom from God's Word

Proverbs 14:12 tells us, "There is a way that seems right to a man, but its end is the way to death." God entrusts you to guide your child to the right path, protecting him as he matures. Proverbs—the book of wisdom—says, "The prudent see danger and take refuge, but the simple keep going and pay the penalty" (Prov. 22:3 NIV). Pray that he will gain the ability to foresee potential dangers and choose wisely.

See these related chapters:
Chapter 10: "Bullying," page 79
Chapter 12: "Cell Phone Struggles," page 89
Chapter 21: "Harmful Habits and Addictions," page 137

Money and Materialism

The money your son, Garrett, borrowed from you—and promised to repay—is now overdue. Recently you learned he also owes his siblings money. Garrett spends his allowance as soon as he gets it. What does he need the extra funds for? The skateboard he "had to have" last month now lies in a dusty corner of the garage . . . next to the fancy sneakers that were so important the month before.

Today, the mother of Garrett's classmate Skylar tells you that Garrett sold Skylar a cheap rhinestone ring by passing it off as real silver and diamonds. Skylar naively believed the slick sales pitch and squandered six months' worth of allowance.

As reality dawns on you, it hurts: Your once-thrifty saver is now a fast talker and spender, convinced that newer is always better and that acquiring money and things is life's highest priority. Garrett's materialism has compromised his savings, his trustworthiness, your family's standards, and his integrity with God.

What Could You Do?

It's been said, "The best time to start talking to your child about money is when he will no longer eat it."[1] Why so early? Because money is one of the most discussed topics in Scripture, and assigning money its proper place is essential.

Here are some ways to help your child turn poor choices about money and possessions into godly ones:

- Determine if your child's attitudes and actions reflect your own values and behavior. If so, ask God to help you model his heart on money and material possessions (Eccles. 5:10 says, "He who loves money will not be satisfied with money, nor he who loves wealth with his income; this also is vanity").
- Tell your child that *everything* we have comes from God and belongs to him. Explain the concept of Christian stewardship, using Matthew 25:14–30 and other biblical texts.
- Share the importance of giving back to God a portion of what God has given. Let your child see you tithe and give offerings. Explain the biblical principle of sowing and reaping (Gal. 6:6–10).
- Train your child to divide his income—from allowance, gifts, chores, etc.—into three categories: spending, savings, and giving. Discuss ideal ratios for each category and where to keep his money (2 Cor. 9:8).
- Model thankfulness for all God has given you and encourage your child to do likewise. At meals or bedtime, encourage family members to name three things they're thankful for (Eph. 5:20; 1 Thess. 5:16–18).
- Let your child help you sponsor a child through a charitable Christian organization. He can write letters to the sponsored child and see how giving has a positive impact on a person his age. He will also learn that others around the world live with far less than he does (Prov. 14:31; 2 Cor. 8:3–5; 1 Tim. 6:17).
- As you give, teach your child to "give bountifully" (2 Cor. 9:6).
- As your child matures, help him open a savings account and set savings goals. Learning delayed gratification will serve your child well. (For more on this, see the Marshmallow Test on pp. 148–49.) Celebrate when the goal is reached.
  - Teach your child to regard savings as well-protected reserves—money accessed in emergency situations or for designated purposes, not for impulsive splurges (Heb. 13:5).

- Explain the concept of credit to your older children and teach them how it should—and shouldn't—be used.
  - Teach your child to look for God's provision when determining God's will. If God wants us to have something, he will provide the means (Deut. 8:17–18).[2]
- Do you buy certain items at particular times of year to get the best price? Clip coupons? Save for retirement? Talk to older children in simple terms about some of the basic concepts involved in your financial decisions, large and small.
- Together, memorize Philippians 4:11: "I have learned in whatever situation I am to be content." Discuss why the *love* of money (not money itself) is the "root of all kinds of evils" (1 Tim. 6:10).

In the case of your son, who cheated his classmate for financial gain, you could also:

- Meet with your child. Affirm your unconditional love for him and your belief in his potential. Ask about the rapid depletion of his savings and his borrowing and spending habits. Draw out his heart and listen carefully for key motivating influences.
- Determine if there have been other instances of passing off inferior goods to earn money.
- Insist that he return the money his classmate paid for the ring, apologize for his deception, and ask forgiveness.
- Direct your child to itemize the money he owes you and all others. Enlist his ideas for repaying his debts and help him create a realistic payment plan.
- Lower his allowance. Then, slowly, as he demonstrates reliability and trustworthiness, allow him to earn more money and greater spending privileges.

What Could You Say?

"I was very proud of you when you [describe a time when your son handled his money responsibly or shared it generously with someone in need]. But lately, I've become concerned over how you think about and handle money.

"Tell me about the ring you sold your classmate." [Listen intently.] "Your friend trusted you, but you chose to break that trust so that you could make money at her expense. Son, how would you feel if you found out the basketball cards you saved up to buy last summer were worthless fakes? And how would you feel about the *person* who sold you those cards?" [Listen and discuss.]

"Tomorrow we're going to your friend's house to return the money she paid you for the ring. While we're there, you'll apologize and ask for forgiveness.

"I also want to discuss your borrowing and spending habits. How much do you owe others?" [Get a precise figure, then continue.] "You've been choosing to spend more than you receive each month—borrowing without repaying so you can buy things you want. This borrowing must stop. A choice to repay what you owe is also a choice to start using the items you've bought with borrowed money. Until then, they're off limits.

"The Bible says we are to live with true contentment with whatever we have, with little or much. Contentment is being satisfied with what we have and not thinking that we always have to have more to be happy. God is our provider. He promises to meet all our *needs*, but not all our *wants*. We honor God when we trust him to provide and thank him as he does.

"If we choose to make money and possessions more important than God, they become idols (Matt. 6:24). They take over the place that God deserves to have in our lives. In Exodus 20:3 God says, 'You shall have no other gods before me.' This includes money and possessions.

"I'd like your thoughts: What are some ways you can please God with your money and possessions? How can you show him that he comes first?" [Listen intently and affirm your child's brainstorming efforts.]

"For a while, I'll oversee more closely how you spend your money. When I see you choosing to think about money and possessions in ways that honor God, your reward will be more freedom—

and a raise in your weekly allowance. God's Word says, 'Whoever can be trusted with very little can also be trusted with much' (Luke 16:10 NIV).

"I love you. And I look forward to seeing you enjoy the blessings that come with handling money wisely and honestly."

Wisdom from God's Word

If you start early to help your child develop a godly perspective on this important issue, it will serve him well for a lifetime. "But godliness with contentment is great gain. For we brought nothing into the world, and we can take nothing out of it. But if we have food and clothing, we will be content with that. Those who want to get rich fall into temptation and a trap and into many foolish and harmful desires that plunge people into ruin and destruction. For the love of money is a root of all kinds of evil. Some people, eager for money, have wandered from the faith and pierced themselves with many griefs. But you, man of God, flee from all this, and pursue righteousness, godliness, faith, love, endurance and gentleness" (1 Tim. 6:6–11 NIV).

See these related chapters:

28

Music Matters

Your daughter, Haley, is outside raking leaves. To say thanks and provide moral support, you bring her a cold drink. As you come up behind your daughter, you hear shocking lyrics blasting through her headphones. You tap her on the shoulder and offer her a bottle of water.

"Thanks, I was thirsty," she says.

"You're working hard! Hey, what's that you're listening to?"

"Stuff I listen to while I work." She smiles and goes back to raking. Heartsick, you walk back into the house, knowing full well—as does your daughter—that the music you heard is morally offensive and unacceptable.

You've given Haley freedom in her music choices because you thought she could handle it. The family rule is that she can listen only to music that would pass her parents' approval. But Haley knows: In no way would you approve of that song! What should you do?

Why Care about Your Child's Music Choices?

Music has a profound impact on the brain and the listener. Even music without words, or words you can't understand, has an effect. *Melodies* evoke emotion. *Lyrics* contain messages. Both can be quickly internalized. So you have several factors to consider when examining your child's music choices.

Realize, as children mature, a great deal of peer pressure centers on music. Likewise, children will show interest in the popular songs that interest their peers. As a parent, your job is to protect your child against harmful messages she may not even be aware she's receiving. Don't be misled if your child says, "I don't listen to the lyrics; I just like the music." The fastest way to memorize words is to set them to a tune. Years, even decades later, we remember the words to songs—they are recorded in our minds through repetition.

Does listening to dark lyrics or heavy metal music mean your child will get involved with drugs or join a gang? Probably not. Those risk-taking behaviors are a result of deeper issues than merely music. Nonetheless, dangerous choices in music can draw immature, naive, and rebellious kids. Be aware of the impact of bullying themes, sexual seduction, and the glorification of rape and suicide. And don't be naïve about the lure of lyrics within evil, occult, and satanic music.

What Could You Do?

It's not a matter of *if* your child will be exposed to unwholesome music but *when*. Screening your child's music is a matter of wise parenting. But there will come a time when your daughter will be in a position to make her own decisions. How can you prepare her to be discerning and self-disciplined?

- Rather than preach about the evils of some music, engage your child's heart in appreciating the fun, motivation, beauty, and inspiration that good music brings to our lives.
- Starting while she's still young, introduce your child to a variety of exemplary music—edifying classics from nearly every genre.
- Carefully choose the music you listen to in the car and at home. Change the station if the content becomes offensive. Your children will notice.

- Designate regular family music nights in your home. Let each person choose a favorite song for everyone in the family to listen to, discuss, and possibly even sing along.
- Talk to your child about the importance of limiting exposure to excessively loud music. When using earbuds or headphones, hearing-loss experts say, "If you cannot understand someone talking to you in a normal speaking voice when they are an arm's length away, [the music] is too loud."[1]
- Equip your child to evaluate the quality of a song's style and words, using Philippians 4:8 as a guide: "Whatever is true, whatever is honorable, whatever is just, whatever is pure, whatever is lovely, whatever is commendable, if there is any excellence, if there is anything worthy of praise, think about these things."
- If your child is old enough to use the Internet, have her supply you with the lyrics to her favorite songs. It's easy to find online information about bands, their lyrics, and what they stand for. Discuss anything problematic. If the music does not meet your standards, eliminate it from the "approved list."
- Make an agreement that for every thirty minutes your child listens to music that falls into the category of "not damaging, but still not something I'm thrilled about," she listens to thirty minutes of something you choose. This isn't about punishment, but rather about exposing your child to composers, musicians, and styles she might not otherwise try. Discuss the impact that various styles of music have on her mind and mood.
- Preapprove playlists on portable music devices. And determine which music stations she may listen to.
- In the tween years, when your daughter likely will prefer music geared toward her generation, steer her to stations that play music already screened for lyrics and lifestyle.
- As in the opening scenario, if your child abuses her privileges by listening to music she knows is off-limits, review the reasons her music is objectionable and confiscate her music device—be it her cell phone, portable music player, etc. When you return it after a designated period for discipline, screen her music choices

even more thoroughly until she demonstrates new habits and trustworthiness.

What Could You Say?

In the case of your daughter, you could say, "Great job raking! You're a hard worker, and I appreciate all that you do to keep our yard looking nice. But we need to talk about the music you were listening to.

"Do you know who listens to all your music with you—even when you're alone?" [Explain how God listens.] "What do the words in that song mean?" [Listen carefully and discuss *why* the lyrics are objectionable.]

"What you listen to matters. Your heart is God's home. The Bible teaches that we become like what we think about (Prov. 23:7). Music can affect your emotions and the way you look at life. If your hands get dirty, you can wash them. But it's a lot harder to wash bad messages out of your mind.

"When you choose to listen to music with harmful lyrics, you're also choosing for me to get more involved in your music decisions. I want you to take a break from using your portable music player for one week. That will give us time to take another look at the bands and lyrics on your playlist. I hope it will also help you appreciate what a privilege it is to have music in your life and to have a say about what you listen to.

"After I return your player, I'll check what you listen to for a while. Then, as you make good choices, you'll receive more freedom over what you listen to and for how long. That's what I wish for you, and I believe it's what you want too. But if you choose to violate the rules again, you'll be choosing not to use your portable devices for two weeks—and I'll monitor your music even more closely when you begin listening again.

"I know you can choose and enjoy music that will build you up, not tear you down. I want you to have fun and enjoy good music. It's one of life's great pleasures!"

Wisdom from God's Word

By setting clear boundaries, you will train your child to infuse her life with uplifting, positive, and encouraging music.

The Bible exhorts us to be discerning about what we allow in our lives . . . and that certainly includes music. Psalm 101:1 says, "I will sing of steadfast love and justice; to you, O LORD, I will make music." "It is my prayer that your love may abound more and more, with knowledge and all discernment, so that you may approve what is excellent, and so be pure and blameless for the day of Christ, filled with the fruit of righteousness that comes through Jesus Christ, to the glory and praise of God" (Phil. 1:9–11).

29

Occult Fascination

You've allowed your son, Colton, to read the first book in an acclaimed children's series, unaware it is filled with occult themes of witchcraft, sorcery, and death. Once you discover these facts, however, you apologize to your son for your oversight, offer to find other books, and tell him he won't be permitted to read the remaining books in the series.

But here it is: Book 2 . . . discovered under his bed as you change his sheets.

Your son is normally compliant and not an avid reader—until now. In fact, recently you've noticed other unusual changes in Colton, including an unquenchable fascination with occult books and comics, video and board games, television and movies . . . all focused on magic, sorcery, and spiritism.

What is this power that seems to have seduced your son? Is it *supernatural* power? What kind of hold does it have?[1]

A Personal Message from June

I need to be candid with you. Until my late twenties I knew nothing about the occult. Then all of a sudden, I felt like a cold, wet washcloth slapped me in the face—and kept slapping!

While preparing to teach a Bible study, I was hit by a tsunami of Scripture. One Scripture after another stunned me—verses I had never seen before—all on the occult. I had no idea God spoke so directly, with so many warnings, about so many activities I thought were innocent. I believed the Bible was mute on the occult, but oh, how wrong I was!

God forbids all avenues into the occult—with the strongest language. Deuteronomy 18:10–12 says, "Let no one be found among you . . . who practices divination or sorcery, interprets omens, engages in witchcraft, or casts spells, or who is a medium or spiritist or who consults the dead. Anyone who does these things is detestable to the LORD" (NIV).

Once I learned how to successfully engage in spiritual warfare, people in occult bondage started coming to me—people who needed to be set free—and many were! Often I would ask, "Do you have anything in your possession that is related to the occult: at home, at work, in your car, anywhere? If so, you must get rid of it."

Obviously, I recognized that the occult has supernatural power, but its source is not God—its source is *the enemy of God*.

In today's culture, kids can be subtly ensnared through likeable literary characters—characters in the media where white magic is used for "good." Wanting to imitate and tap into powers that appear "fun," kids can easily fall prey to darkness disguised as light.

That's why this chapter is so important.

What Is the Occult and How Does It Entice Our Kids?

The occult refers to any object or practice used in an "attempt to gain supernatural knowledge or power apart from the God of the Bible."[2] Each item and practice promises to divulge something *hidden* to their disciples. In fact, the word *occult* means "hidden." Since curiosity about forbidden things is a human trait, *natural curiosity* is the "hook" that occultists use to lure children and adults alike—the deceived who are unaware of the destructive hidden dangers.

"What's wrong with the occult?" your child may ask. The number one answer is: "God is against the occult because its power source is Satan." Make no mistake, involvement in the occult opens a door into a realm clearly forbidden by God. In Leviticus 20:6–7 the Lord says, "I will set my face against anyone who turns to mediums and spiritists to prostitute themselves by following them, and I will cut them off from their people. Consecrate yourselves and be holy [set apart for God], because I am the LORD your God" (NIV).

What Could You Do?

* Research the answers to key questions your kids or your kids' friends might ask.[3] In reality, many people, even Christians, don't know what the Bible says about the occult. For example:
  - *"What's wrong with séances and trying to talk to dead people?"* The Bible explains that people need to go to God, who is all-powerful, *not* to a counterfeit who is taking the place of God. The Bible says, "When someone tells you to consult mediums and spiritists, who whisper and mutter, should not a people inquire of their God? Why consult the dead on behalf of the living?" (Isa. 8:19 NIV).
  - *"What about reading horoscopes?"* The Bible says *don't!* The message is clear about horoscopes and astrology: "Learn not the way of the nations, nor be dismayed at the signs of the heavens because the nations are dismayed at them" (Jer. 10:2).
  - *"What is the matter with witchcraft or casting spells?"* The Lord reveals the end of both occult practices: "I will destroy your witchcraft and you will no longer cast spells" (Mic. 5:12 NIV).
  - *"What's wrong with going to mediums or spiritists out of curiosity to see what they say?"* This practice is not only forbidden by God, but it also opens the door to being deceived and influenced by demons. The Bible clearly states, "Do not turn to mediums or seek out spiritists, for you will be defiled by them" (Lev. 19:31 NIV).

- *"What about using magic charms for protection?"* The charms forbidden here are not endearing charms found on charm bracelets, but magic good luck charms (like rabbits' feet) that are ascribed supernatural power. God again gives the answer: "I am against your magic charms with which you ensnare people like birds and I will tear them from your arms" (Ezek. 13:20 NIV).
- Recognize warning signs in your child's clothing, makeup, writing, and demeanor.
  - Note any dark, dramatic changes: all black clothing, heavy dark makeup, secret activities, or sullen friends.
  - Pay attention to your child's doodling. Look for distorted crosses, hexagrams, depictions of Diana and Lucifer, and symbols for Satan, including the inverted pentagram, horn-hand, 666 or FFF, and mark of the beast.
- Review what your son is reading and watching—his books and comics, video and board games, movies and music—for any openings into the occult. Filter what your child is exposed to in order to "refuse the evil and choose the good" (Isa. 7:15 NKJV).
- Realize that your son's friends may innocently introduce him to the occult. Get to know his friends and their families—their faith, values, and priorities. "Do not be misled: 'Bad company corrupts good character'" (1 Cor. 15:33 NIV).
- Remove all objects related to the occult from your home. Destroy all occult-related items, including those with zodiac signs. "A number of those who had practiced magic arts brought their books together and burned them in the sight of all" (Acts 19:19).
- Renounce any involvement with the occult. Teach your son by example the importance of turning away from, fighting against, and refusing to have anything to do with the occult: "Many of those who were now believers came, confessing and divulging their practices" (Acts 19:18).
- Read about spiritual warfare. Be prepared to share with your son what *spiritual warfare* means. Use words and images he can understand. Remind him where the strength to win this spiritual war originates: "Finally, be strong in the Lord and in the strength

of his might. Put on the whole armor of God, that you may be able to stand against the schemes of the devil" (Eph. 6:10–11).

- Resolve, if your son is involved in the occult, to do whatever it takes to get him out. Contact knowledgeable Christian ministries, such as HOPE FOR THE HEART, to provide the resources needed to help eliminate the occult's influence on your family. Notice the words of the apostle Paul: "Be humble when you are trying to teach those who are mixed up concerning the truth. For if you talk meekly and courteously to them, they are more likely, with God's help, to turn away from their wrong ideas and believe what is true. Then they will come to their senses and escape from Satan's trap of slavery to sin, which he uses to catch them whenever he likes, and then they can begin doing the will of God" (2 Tim. 2:25–26 TLB).

- Repent and ask your family's forgiveness for any area where you've compromised. Also, lead your child in asking forgiveness. The Bible says, "Bear with each other and forgive one another if any of you has a grievance against someone. Forgive as the Lord forgave you" (Col. 3:13 NIV).

- Rely on the supreme authority over evil. Together, as a family, memorize 1 John 4:4: "The one [Christ] who is in you is greater than the one [the Enemy] who is in the world" (NIV).

What Could You Say?

When talking to your son about the dangers of the occult, you could say, "God gave you a mind that's curious and I thank God for that. God can use your curiosity to help you get to know him and to make your life better. But you've shown an interest in something very dark and dangerous and your interest is so strong that you're willing to disobey me." [Hold up the book you found.]

"These books may seem innocent, but they're part of the occult, which tries to get special knowledge or power apart from the God of the Bible. His Word tells us *not* to do this. By reading these books, you are opening yourself to the occult—even without meaning to—and you can invite evil spirits into your life that could hurt you. This means you can miss out on God's best for your life.

"God loves you. He would never want to keep you from enjoying something that's good for you. Psalm 84:11 says, 'No good thing does he withhold from those who walk uprightly.' But you're not allowed to read [name of the series] books.

"If you choose to read anything similar, you're making a choice for me to pick every single book, song, television show, and game for you *and* when you can have them. But if you choose to obey, you'll be choosing more freedom to make your own selections.

"God has more power than anyone or anything. He's the original source of all the *best* adventure, mystery, beauty, and power. No witch or sorcerer could ever compare with him.

"I love you, son, and I want you to learn all you can about God and how to use his power to make you the person he created you to be. I'm excited about your interest in reading books. And we're going to find some that will line up your thinking with God's thinking. Let's pray and ask God to guide us."

Wisdom from God's Word

Scripture makes it crystal clear: "Satan himself masquerades as an angel of light" (2 Cor. 11:14 NIV). The occult is deceptive and dangerous. Only trouble and despair await those who participate in it, as Scripture warns: "Woe to those who call evil good and good evil, who put darkness for light and light for darkness, who put bitter for sweet and sweet for bitter!" (Isa. 5:20).

Ultimately, regardless of how much or little exposure we personally have to the occult, we can take the action steps mentioned in the Bible: "We have renounced secret and shameful ways; we do not use deception, nor do we distort the word of God" (2 Cor. 4:2 NIV).*

See these related chapters:
Chapter 26: "Media Mania," page 164
Chapter 28: "Music Matters," page 175

---

* Further information on the occult and spiritual warfare is available from www.hopefortheheart.org.

30

Peer Pressure

Your son, Austin, is hosting a sleepover. The two of you have discussed the evening's activities, and he's selected two movies—from a group you've preapproved—for after-dinner viewing. A few minutes after the second movie starts, you decide to surprise the boys with an extra plate of homemade cookies. However, a conversation you overhear as you approach the den stops you in your tracks.

"This movie's boring. C'mon, let's watch the one I brought."

After a pause, your son answers, "No, my parents only let me watch PG movies."

"Who cares?" the friend presses. "I heard this one's awesome."

"Yeah," another guest chimes in. "It's not like your parents have to know."

Holding your breath, you wonder, *What will Austin choose when pressured by peers?* When the movie's theme music begins . . . you have your answer.

What Could You Do?

While your preschooler will likely view *you* as the center of his universe, your school-age child will increasingly be influenced by his peers. As he matures and seeks to become his own person, he'll alternately push you away emotionally then draw you close. This is normal. Your child is redefining his social boundaries.[1] In the midst of these seismic shifts, remain consistent with your presence and guidance. It's also important to:

- Discreetly stay attuned to your child's social life without elbowing your way into the center of it. While aware that you keep an eye on him, he'll respect your sensitivity to his growing need for independence. If you exert undue oversight now, you risk being perceived as someone to hide things from.

- Talk with your child about what peer pressure is and how it works. Use role-playing to help him discern improper peer influence. Then help him learn ways to positively influence his friends.

- Create a home environment that encourages calm, candid dialogue, instills responsibility and integrity, and models a well-defined sense of right and wrong.

- Know your child's friends and be involved in his everyday world so you can evaluate his actions and attitudes firsthand.
  - As much as possible, volunteer to help with extracurricular activities, school events, carpooling, etc.
  - Make your home a gathering place for group activities—a fun spot for your child and his friends to congregate.
  - Befriend the parents of your child's friends.

- Expand your child's freedom as he displays trustworthiness with peers. Conversely, if he begins making unwise choices, tighten boundaries until you see growth. (This process will need to be repeated throughout childhood.)

- Talk with your child about how the children of Israel suffered after demanding a human king so they could be like all the other nations (beginning in 1 Samuel 8).
  - Discuss how Christ, throughout the Gospels, responded to pressure from the Pharisees.
  - Discuss how the apostle Peter hypocritically adjusted his eating habits to appease his peers (Gal. 2:11–14).

- Together, study notable individuals throughout history, such as Abraham Lincoln, who did the good and godly thing, despite fierce peer pressure.

- Stage group activities such as movie-watching in *public* areas of your home. (See chap. 26 "Media Mania" on p. 164.)

What Could You Say?

In the case of your son, who gave in to peer pressure by his movie choice, you could enter the room and, as you eject the movie, calmly say, "Hey, guys, I'm sure this is an exciting movie, but we don't watch movies that aren't age-appropriate and preapproved. I made some cookies, and you can play a board game and eat while you play!"

During the course of the game, casually ask questions to get the boys thinking and talking. "What is it about the movie that made you want to watch it? Why do you think it has that rating? If you feed your mind a diet of things that aren't good for it, what do you think will happen before long?" [Discuss their ideas and add your own.]

After his friends go home, talk with your son, using open-ended questions (ones that can't be answered *yes* or *no*) to draw him out. "Since you know our rule about movie ratings, why did you decide to watch the movie?" [Listen carefully to his responses.] "How did you feel inside about breaking our rule? What do you think would've happened if you had said *no*?

"Throughout life, you'll feel pressure to go along with the crowd—from what to wear to the words you use to how you treat others. This is called 'peer pressure.' Peers are the people you hang out with.

"What matters most is that you act the same way when I'm looking as you act when you think no one's looking. Because the truth is, God is always looking. Hebrews 4:13 says, 'Nothing in all creation is hidden from God's sight. Everything is uncovered and laid bare before the eyes of him to whom we must give account' (NIV).

"The Lord created you and set you apart for a special purpose. He'll bring friends into your life who need him. They'll look to you to give them an idea of what God is like and what's important to him. You have a choice to make. Will you reflect God's character to them by doing what he would do? Or will you cave in to peer pressure? If you do, they'll see you as weak and lose respect for you . . . and for God.' And you will lose respect for yourself. But if you set a good example, they'll respect you. And they'll have a clearer choice about who they want to be like.

"Here's a simple test to give yourself anytime you face a tough choice:

1. If I do it, will I feel bad? (Would I hide it from my parents?)
2. How would I feel if everyone knew I did it? (Would I mind if everyone saw it on TV?)
3. Does it line up with what I already know is right or wrong? (Would Jesus want me to do it?)

"If you know it's wrong, don't do it. If you're not sure, ask.[2]

"Anytime you feel you must hide what you're doing, it's a sign you're not making a wise choice. The Bible says, 'Am I now trying to win the approval of human beings, or of God? Or am I trying to please people? If I were still trying to please people, I would not be a servant of Christ' (Gal. 1:10 NIV). We're going to memorize that Scripture together.

"When you chose to break our family's boundary about movies, you also chose the repercussion. In this case, you won't watch movies until you can tell me the test questions and explain how they'll help you make wise choices in the future.

"What are some words you could use next time to say *no* to something your friends want to do but that you know is wrong? Let's pretend I'm your friend so we can talk it through." [Role-play the scenario with your son.]

"The reward for saying *no* when friends try to get you to do something wrong is a clear conscience and the blessing of God. There are other rewards, too, like self-respect, the respect of your friends, and increased freedom as I see you making wise choices. I believe that's what you want, and it's what I want for you. It's your choice. I know you can do it!"

Wisdom from God's Word

Pray for your child to have friends who are wise. The Bible says, "Whoever walks with the wise becomes wise, but the companion of fools will suffer harm" (Prov. 13:20). Everyone experiences peer pressure, but the heart focused on God finds peace, stability, and belonging.

Choosing friends is a vital life skill, but even more important is choosing to follow Christ. "The fear of man lays a snare, but whoever trusts in the LORD is safe" (Prov. 29:25).

See these related chapters:
Chapter 13: "Cheating," page 95
Chapter 24: "Lying," page 152
Chapter 26: "Media Mania," page 164

Procrastination

Your poor puppy, Bo, is so dirty and so desperate for a bath that he's pawing at his nose in protest. Rather than handing out clothes pins for your family's noses, you strategize ways to motivate your son to give his four-pawed pal a long overdue wash.

You'd hoped the multiple reminders would have moved your son to get into gear long before now. But your main concern transcends dirt on the dog—Matt waits until the last minute to handle almost *every* responsibility. Even his soccer coach remarked, "Matt's a talented kid . . . once he decides to get moving."

So, how do you get your young procrastinator to *produce*?

Why Do Children Procrastinate?

Do you recognize your child in one (or more) of these five profiles?[1]

Perfectionist Patty. Since she knows she can't always do everything perfectly, Perfectionist Patty procrastinates to prevent even the possibility of imperfection.

Poor Self-Worth Paul. To avoid revealing perceived inadequacies, Poor Self-Worth Paul puts off starting.

Fear-Based Freddie. Fear of harsh judgment affects Fear-Based Freddie's confidence and trust in others. He procrastinates to avoid people and responsibilities, as well as his fear of failure.

Lack-of-Goals Larry. If Lack-of-Goals Larry isn't required to establish and stick to goals, he will procrastinate because he has no clear motivation, direction, or focus.

Overwhelmed Olivia. When Overwhelmed Olivia becomes overloaded by her responsibilities, she doesn't know where to start. Rather than giving the most important tasks top priority, she gravitates toward easier tasks.

What Could You Do?

- Be sure the tasks you assign are age appropriate.
- Nurture your child's God-given instinct to be independent. Procrastination often develops from "learned helplessness."
- At first, teach your child how to do the job by working alongside him. Once a task is mastered, resist doing for your child what he can do for himself. Otherwise he learns to avoid doing a job because he knows you will eventually step in and do it.
- Encourage your child to take the first step of a task and praise him when he does. Starting a project—overcoming inertia—can build confidence and momentum.
- Praise your child's efforts, not just his accomplishments.
- A child may delay starting an activity because he's trained himself to function better under deadline pressure. Help him reprogram his "normal" to start projects sooner and work steadily rather than starting at the last minute and working furiously. Demonstrate how this approach allows time to compensate for the unexpected.
- Gently coach your child to build self-confidence, assuring him that he is able to meet challenges.
- Follow up if your child delays after being asked to do something. If a distraction has captured his attention (television, video games, etc.), remove it until he completes the task.
- A procrastinator often has a poor sense of the amount of time required to do a job. Help your child practice setting realistic schedules to achieve his goals. Build in periods for rest and play.
- Limit recreational activities—video games, movies, television, computer use, etc.—that distract your child from more im-

portant activities. Let these activities be rewards for a job well done. (See chap. 26 "Media Mania" on p. 164.)

- Set an example by structuring a family life that balances rest and leisure time with productivity.
- Your child may justify procrastination with excuses: "None of the other kids my age have to [fill in the blank]. It's not fair." If your child still complains after you assure him that his task is age appropriate, add another responsibility.
- Suspend your child's allowance. Explain that once he chooses to finish his chores on time for an entire week (without being reminded) he'll receive his allowance again.
- Recognize and encourage work that is done well and on time.

In addition, consider the following specialized strategies tailored to the underlying cause of your child's individual procrastination problem:

- Help *Perfectionist Patty* learn to enjoy her work. Remind her that Jesus alone is perfect and that her job is to aim for excellence, not perfection. Help her see that honest mistakes help us grow. Praise her efforts, not just her outcomes. Together, memorize Hebrews 10:36: "You need to keep on patiently doing God's will if you want him to do for you all that he has promised" (TLB).
- Help *Poor Self-Worth Paul* brainstorm a list of his strengths and abilities. Then match those qualities to the steps he will need to take to complete his project. Together memorize Philippians 4:13: "I can do all things through Christ who strengthens me" (NKJV).
- Help *Fear-Based Freddie* identify what he fears. Assure him that, often, courage is feeling afraid, yet doing what needs to be done anyway. Together, memorize Deuteronomy 31:8: "The LORD himself goes before you and will be with you; he will never leave you nor forsake you. Do not be afraid; do not be discouraged." Afterward, further assure him. He'll be glad he did and will find great satisfaction and fulfillment.
- Help *Lack-of-Goals Larry* choose goals that are SMART: Specific, Measurable, Attainable, Realistic, and Time-Sensitive.[2]

Celebrate when he accomplishes a goal. Then help him set another one. Together, memorize Proverbs 21:5: "The plans of the diligent lead to profit" (NIV).

• Help *Overwhelmed Olivia* learn to identify her three top priorities each day. Then show her how to break each task into manageable steps. After she accomplishes each portion, she can cross it off her list. Remind her that families work together as a team and that she may ask for help when she needs it. Encourage her to keep her focus on "first things first." Together, memorize Proverbs 4:25: "Let your eyes look directly forward, and your gaze be straight before you."

What Could You Say?

In the case of your son, who puts off washing the family mascot, you could say, "Son, I appreciated the way you [describe a previous time when he tackled a task on time]. So I know you can do a good job and do it on time. But you've put off washing poor Bo all weekend, even after I've reminded you. It's time to get the wash tub out of the garage, get the soap, scrubbing brush, and towels from the utility room, and give Bo a bath. Now!

"If you start right now, you'll be finished before dinner and be able to go to your friend's sleepover. You have a choice. If you choose not to wash Bo before dinner, you'll be choosing to stay home and miss the sleepover tonight." [If this is a repeat offense, you could add, "A choice not to wash Bo before dinner is also a choice not to watch television or play video games tonight."]

"Putting off what you're supposed to do can keep you from doing your best work and using your best ideas. It can cause you to carry around guilt and stress that God did not intend and you can easily avoid. You can also run out of time and have to pay a penalty, depending on what you have put off doing.

"Tell me, what could you do differently to start on time when you have a job to do? Is there something I can do to help?

"I know that in your heart, you want to please me and you want Bo to be happy and clean. And what's more important, I know you want to please the Lord, too, by taking care of your chores and doing them on time. Once you start a project you give such a good effort, and that makes me very proud. I believe you can do the same thing today. I'm cheering for you!"

Wisdom from God's Word

When your slow starter struggles to overcome his pattern of procrastination, remind him of the result. The apostle Paul said, "Do you not know that in a race all the runners run, but only one gets the prize? Run in such a way as to get the prize" (1 Cor. 9:24 NIV). And probably the best prize for overcoming procrastination is peace—inner peace.

See these related chapters:
Chapter 8: "Bedtime Battles," page 71
Chapter 14: "Chores," page 99
Chapter 39: "Tardiness," page 230

32

Profanity and Name-Calling

On the sidelines, you watch your son's basketball game, proud of his steady athletic progress. But when an opponent knocks Brock out of bounds, you're shocked when the referee gives your son a technical foul for bad language.

What? Bad language? Brock?

After the game, you ask Brock about the incident.

"So what?" he shrugs. "Everybody says that!"

"Everybody?"

"Kids at school . . . kids on the team. What's the big deal?"

How can you help your child stop using bad language before it becomes a habit?

What Could You Do?

- Toddlers learn to speak by imitating what they hear. If you yourself use bad language, you're demonstrating a level of disrespect and dishonor which is likely to be copied by your impressionable son. So start now: Set a good example through *your* speech.

- Recognize that language can be fun and freeing. Capitalize on your child's immense capacity for building vocabulary. As he grows, explain the origin and meaning of interesting words, helping him build a rich repertoire.

- Use concise, descriptive language, and your child will follow suit. Explain that words have both denotations and connotations. Encourage him to find the appropriate word for what he thinks and feels.
- Children often absorb what's being said through television and music. Even if a theme is over their heads, they recognize and repeat many of the spoken words. Monitor their choices accordingly. (See chap. 26 "Media Mania" on p. 164 and chap. 28 "Music Matters" on p. 175.)
- Ensure that your child understands which words are out of bounds and why. Include hurtful phrases such as "I hate you" and "You're a stupid idiot." Aimed to wound, these words can be just as damaging as profanity.
- Explain the power of spoken words, as described in James 3:2–12.
- With your child, memorize Ephesians 4:29.
- To boost awareness and self-control, help your child replace inappropriate words and phrases with ones that don't attack others and aren't offensive to God.
- When your child uses profanity or hateful words, require him to apologize to those who heard it. Additionally, have your younger child choose three better words he can use. Have an older child think of twice that many.
- Resist the urge to overreact or shame your child when he uses bad language unknowingly at an embarrassing time or place. Instead, calmly ask, "What's a better way to say that?"
- For stubborn repeat offenders, have your child wash his mouth out with . . . Scripture!
  - Start by explaining, "It's not what goes into your mouth that defiles you; you are defiled by what comes out of your mouth" (Matt. 15:11 NLT).
  - Share how God's Word will wash us on the inside, like soap washes us on the outside (Eph. 5:26).
  - Select a number of Scriptures about speech and the power of the tongue, and set aside an age-appropriate amount of time for your child to spend reciting those verses.

– After each verse, instruct your child to explain what he heard and how it applies to his word choices.

What about "Potty Talk"?

Young children have a penchant for words about private bodily functions. From burping to passing gas, laughing about bodily sounds and functions rarely gets old. If simply ignoring the behavior during this fleeting phase doesn't work, tell your child not to talk publicly about bodily functions and offer appropriate words for him to use.

What Could You Say?

In the case of your son, who used profanity during the basketball game, you could say, "Son, I'm proud of how you give your best effort in basketball. You listen to your coach and stay focused. But when you were knocked out of bounds, I was shocked and disappointed by the words you chose to say. And I'm especially concerned you didn't see anything wrong with saying them.

"Words are important. They have the power to build others up or to tear them down. They also reflect what's in your heart. People get an idea of what kind of person you are from your words. People get hurt by ugly words, and they won't want to be your friend when you use them.

"The referee did the right thing when he removed you from the game. You, and you alone, are in charge of what comes out of your mouth.

"The Bible says, 'Let no one despise you for your youth, but set the believers an example in *speech,* in conduct, in love, in faith, in purity.' I'd like your thoughts on what that means." [Discuss 1 Tim. 4:12.] "Were your words an example of purity?

"When you said what you did at the game, what were you thinking? What were you feeling?" [Wait for an answer and clarification.] "Now, let me hear you practice saying how you felt, using words that honor yourself and God.

"Because you chose to use bad words during the game, you'll need to apologize to the referee. After that, we're going home so you can spend time thinking and writing about what you will do and say the next time you get angry at a game. You may not stay to watch the next game.

"I'm going to talk to your coach tomorrow. If you choose to use bad language in the future, you'll also be choosing to sit out the following game and not to go out with your team for pizza.

"I know you can speak without using bad words, even when you're frustrated. When you do, your reward will be getting to play on the team, pleasing God, setting a good example for the little kids who are watching you, feeling good about yourself, and building a good reputation. I believe that's what you want, and that's what I want for you.

"Listen to the heart of 1 Timothy 4:12: 'Let no one despise you for your youth, but set the believers an example in speech, in conduct, in love, in faith, in purity.'"

Wisdom from God's Word

Words have tremendous power. Creation came into being by virtue of God's Word (see Genesis 1). The Bible also tells us "the tongue has the power of life and death" (Prov. 18:21 NIV). God instructs us to speak encouragement, admonishment, instruction, and hope. And Psalm 19:14 teaches us to pray, "Let the words of my mouth and the meditation of my heart be acceptable in your sight, O LORD, my rock and my redeemer."

See these related chapters:
Chapter 17: "Disrespectfulness," page 117
Chapter 26: "Media Mania," page 164
Chapter 28: "Music Matters," page 175

33

Sexual Curiosity

After dinner, family friends linger around the table for dessert and conversation. Getting up to make coffee, you decide to check on the children. When the meal ended, your daughter, Mary, and your friend's son, Aiden, ran off to play, and now you remember one of the basic principles of parenting: If it's too quiet *investigate*. Entering your child's bedroom, you discover Mary and Aiden, half-dressed, curiously comparing their private parts.

Oh my! How do I address this?

Why Do Young Children Explore Their Bodies?

Children are naturally curious. Babies discover their hands, and we smile. They find their toes, and we laugh. They take note of their genitals, and . . . many a parent feels vaguely unnerved. In truth, there's no need for discomfort. The human body, including its reproductive parts, is an expression of God's marvelous creativity and design.

Children may see each other's private parts when they are young, such as when dressing or bathing. In today's world, however, natural curiosity often is stirred prematurely as tender minds are exposed to sexually explicit pictures, words, music, and advertisements (see chap. 26, "Media Mania" on p. 164). Therefore, it's important to know that:

- Children need to learn about sexuality in age-appropriate ways, and they need to learn it—first and foremost—from their parents.
- Learning about sexuality from peers or the media can cause confusion because of misinformation.
- Without instruction and information, young children do not perceive that one body part requires greater modesty and discretion than others.
- Parents have a glorious opportunity to teach that the sexual relationship is a gift from God intended for marriage between a husband and wife. From the love they share with one another, through a miracle of God, babies are created.

What Could You Do?

- Convey to your child that God created each part of the body for a special purpose. Certain parts of the body (those covered by a modest swimsuit) are private and are to be seen only by parents for health reasons and occasionally by a family doctor for medical reasons.
- Instruct your child in an age-appropriate way not to touch other people's private parts. Additionally, tell your child that if someone wants to touch hers, she must firmly refuse and inform you immediately.
- Your example is *key*. Dress modestly around the house. Parental nudity, even around children of the same sex, can send a mixed message when you are hoping to teach the importance of covering your private parts. When parents model modesty, children are more likely to follow suit.
- Don't shame your child for expressing natural curiosity.
- Review Christian resources that will help you teach your young child about sex in age-appropriate ways.[1]
- From an early age, designate bedrooms for sleeping and common areas—living and family rooms—for playing. Children will find far less opportunity for sexual exploration when playing in the family's sight.

Children may stimulate themselves sexually without realizing what they're doing. Avoid criticism and overreaction. As with most things, this exploratory activity is usually nothing more than a passing stage. Distract your child and move through it with grace and gentle guidance.

One parent tells of walking into her three-year-old's bedroom after his nap to discover him naked, fondling his genitals. To this new mom's surprise, her son had an erection. Rather than expressing shock, she casually said, "Honey, let's get your clothes on and go play in the yard."

With the distraction, the erection went away. Dismayed, the boy exclaimed, "Oh, no! Now it's broken!" Stifling a smile, the mother assured her son that his body would continue to work just as God intended. Since the child didn't see the erection as a sexual activity, the mother wisely didn't launch into a talk about sex. She calmly gave her son the information he needed and moved on.

Occasionally a child will show continued interest in sexual behavior and self-stimulation. If efforts to redirect and distract are not successful and the behavior becomes compulsive, consult with a qualified therapist.

In the case of your daughter, who was exploring private parts with a friend's son after dinner, bring the children back into the room with the family and discreetly inform the other child's parents so they, too, can follow up with appropriate attention once they're home.

What Could You Say?

After your dinner guests leave, you could say, "Sweetie, I sure had fun tonight visiting with Aiden and his parents. Did you have a nice time?" [Listen.] "When you had your panties down in the bedroom, what were you and Aiden doing?"

You may get a simple answer like, "Aiden said he gets to stand up to go potty. He showed me how. But I don't look the same. How come?"

From there, merely answer the question being asked. "God made boys and girls differently. Aiden is a boy, and boys have a penis. You and I are girls. Girls have a vagina instead of a penis. Girls sit down to potty. If we stood up, we'd get the seat wet."

That's it. There's no need to launch into Sexual Behavior 101.

However, do explain, "The places our swimsuits cover are our *private parts*. What does your swimsuit cover?" [Let your child show you and name the parts as she does.] "Only your parents and our doctor may see your private parts. If someone else wants to see them, you say, 'No! This is private!' And then tell me what happened right away. Let's practice saying that." [Do so.]

For a child old enough to know better (and that age will vary depending on your child), you could add: "If you choose to show your private parts again to Aiden or look at his, you'll also be choosing not to play together for a while—until I can be sure you'll respect each other's private parts. I believe you'll do the right thing."

For children who touch their genitals beyond personal hygiene needs, you could say, "We clean the parts of our body covered by our swimsuits just like we clean the rest of our body. But we don't spend extra time touching our private parts." If asked why, you could say, "These parts have a special purpose for mommies and daddies to share after they get married. I'll tell you more about that when you're older."

Wisdom from God's Word

The Song of Solomon tells us again and again "not to awaken love until the time is right" (2:7; 3:5; 8:4 NLT). Even when your child is too young to comprehend God's heart on the priority of sexual purity, you can plant seeds that will bear fruit now and throughout her life.

See Chapter 34: "Sexual Storms," page 204

34

Sexual Storms

For the last couple of days, your daughter, Zoe, has been walking home from the school bus with the next-door neighbor boy. From the window today, you saw the two coming down the driveway right on time.

Locating your keys, you go outside to usher Zoe and her brother into the car to drive to their dentist appointment. What a shock to find your daughter and the neighbor boy behind the garage—kissing! And you're not happy to see where his hands are placed.

Stuffing your shock, you send the boy on his way and manage to point the car in the right direction. Just as you're about to launch into a lecture, your daughter speaks up.

"I don't know what you're upset about. Everyone is doing it!"

Doing it? Everyone?

What Influences Sexual Awareness?

Instead of seeing relationships that chastely grow and mature as couples get to know one another, today's kids are exposed, at every turn, to couples focusing on the physical and casually jumping into sexual involvement.

For girls: The core desire of a little girl is to be loved with a perfect love. From her circle of relationships, a girl looks for approval, affirmation, acceptance, and the reassurance that she's beautiful.[1]

The disappearance of morality in current culture can send girls careening into the adult world of sexuality before they're emotionally equipped. Sexualized images of females in advertising, merchandising, and media harm the development of a girl's sexual self-image.[2] When the world insists that females be thin, sexy, and outwardly beautiful, it's easy for girls to look to the mirror—and to the reaction of boys—to determine their worth.

This sexual objectification undermines a girl's confidence and comfort with her own body and can trigger shame, anxiety, eating disorders, low self-esteem, and depression, and further inhibit development of a healthy sexual image.[3]

For boys: It's common for boys to receive the cultural message that they can prove their manhood by becoming sexually active early. And, yes, a double standard exists. When a boy talks about sexual things and acts in sexual ways, by worldly standards he often is considered a "stud." However, a girl who behaves similarly may be labeled a "slut."[4] For boys, delving into pornography is frequently viewed as a rite of passage, when in reality it's a dark and dangerous path toward a distorted view of themselves and of women.[5]

It's been said that boys touch first with their eyes and then with their hands. When girls display their bodies through revealing clothing, boys—especially in the absence of godly instruction and mentoring—may consider this an invitation, and girls misinterpret the resulting attention as love.

What Could You Do?

- Recognize that you are the best, most qualified sex-education teacher for your child.
- Exemplify sexual purity in your own life.
- At an early age, introduce your daughter to Jesus and help her get to know him as the greatest love of her life—the one who fully knows and loves her and the one she should want to please foremost.

- Teach your child the biblical meaning of *agape* love (God's love, which seeks the very best for the person loved). As she matures, help her think about how to practice this type of love in opposite-sex relationships.
- Focus on your child's strengths and interests, helping her develop a sense of worth through the confidence that she is created in God's image and is uniquely gifted (Ps. 139:14).
- Help your child understand that true acceptance comes through embracing her identity in Christ.
- Teach a biblical view of male and female roles as joint heirs in Christ and that one gender is not better than the other.

• Teach your child that sexual activity is a gift reserved for husbands and wives—a gift not to be opened early, for then it will surely be misused.

• Talk candidly with your child about sex and sexual purity as questions arise. Keep responses developmentally appropriate, according to maturity level.

• If she asks a simple question, give a simple, straight-forward reply. If the question is more involved, give a more detailed reply.

• Help your child find a community of like-minded kids committed to a common standard of sexual purity.

• Discourage your child from developing exclusive relationships (boyfriend/girlfriend or "going steady") with the opposite sex.

• Define what words are appropriate and which ones are not. If your child is using inappropriate sexual words, explain their meanings and why they aren't to be part of her vocabulary.

• Guide your daughters to be ladies and your sons to be gentlemen, accustomed to being treated—and treating others—with dignity and respect.

• Train your child to keep her eyes and thoughts on what is good and pure, to avoid pornography and sexual fantasies (Phil. 4:8), and to "stay away from all sexual sin. Then each of you will control his own body and live in holiness and honor—not in lustful passion like the pagans who do not know God and his ways" (1 Thess. 4:3–5 NLT).

What Could You Do for Daughters?

- Talk with your daughter about the natural desire for the love of a young man. Assure her that, should marriage be part of God's wonderful plan for her life, the time for appropriate sexual relations will come when she is older. For right now, however, her focus should be on resting in God's timing as she learns, matures, explores life and relationships, and enjoys the gift of childhood.
- Through Bible study, guide your daughter to see her identity as the beloved and cherished daughter of the King of kings.
- With your daughter, attend a conference or church retreat designed specifically to help girls live virtuous lives. Read related children's book series to reinforce these godly principles.[6]

What Could You Do for Sons?

- Give your son a healthy view of women as sisters and joint heirs with Christ.[7]
- Train your son to treat his mother and all other females with honor and respect.
- Encourage your son to use his strength for noble purposes, rooted in a heart of service and respect.
- Instruct your son to honor and protect the reputation and purity of all girls.
- Through Bible study, guide your son to see his identity as a beloved, mighty man of God.[8]

What Could You Say?

In the case of your daughter, who was caught kissing the neighbor boy, you could say, "You're growing up and your body and emotions are changing. It feels exciting to be touched and kissed. Kissing excites sexual desire and passion. That's by God's design!

"But stirring up sexual feelings when you're young is like opening your Christmas gift in September. God designed marriage as the setting to open his gift of sex. He intends marriage to provide the security of a lifelong commitment. Until then, the Lord tells us to be sexually pure. That means we honor God and ourselves by keeping our bodies private and by not doing things, or dwelling on thoughts, that would arouse sexual feelings.

"I realize this may go against what others do and what you may hear. The world's view of sex is pretty much the opposite of God's view. He says, 'Guard your heart' (Prov. 4:23 NIV)."

[In advance, make a paper heart with your daughter's name written on it. Present the heart, and continue.]

"Your heart and your body are *very* much connected. Trying to separate them so you can give your body without your heart is impossible. God intends your whole body and whole heart to be given to your husband in marriage. Until then, you're to protect your heart and body so you can experience true love God's way.

"Imagine giving part of your body and heart to your neighborhood friend [as you say this, tear off a piece of the heart and let it fall to the ground]. Next year, you give another part to another boy [tear off another piece of the heart] . . . and another [off comes another piece of the paper heart]. By the time you are old enough to get married, what would be left to offer your husband?" [Allow your daughter to share her observations about what's left of the shredded heart.]

"You can ask me anything anytime about your body, your feelings, and about sex. I'll give you honest answers. Don't rely on your friends or movies for information about sex because you can get a lot of wrong information.

"Together we'll establish boundaries that will help you stay safe and sexually pure. What ideas do you have that will keep you from situations where you're tempted to become sexually involved?" [Listen and explore ideas.]

"I'm going to speak with [name of the boy your daughter was

kissing] and his parents. If you both choose to practice godly boundaries and behavior, you may continue to be friends. Otherwise, you'll be choosing to end the friendship.

"I love you and care deeply for your heart, and God does too! He's created you perfectly for his purpose. He's also established a timetable to transition into becoming a grown-up. Sex is wonderful and unique—and set aside for when you're married. Together, we'll protect that 'wedding gift' until it's ready to open."

Wisdom from God's Word

The world bombards children with sexual images and language. Your home is the arena to combat misinformation with healthy discussions based on God's Word and his plan for sex in marriage.

"Flee from sexual immorality. Every other sin a person commits is outside the body, but the sexually immoral person sins against his own body" (1 Cor. 6:18).

See these related chapters:

35

Sibling Rivalry and Selfishness

You have childhood memories of competing with your siblings over almost everything, from who could run the fastest to who could outsmart the other. Then and there you vow that when you have your own children, they won't endure the same battles. Your kids will be best buddies . . . *yeah, right.*

Your oldest, Karl, continually claims the most comfortable chair, the largest dessert, and first use of all toys and games. Your second, Kent, wears a perpetual scowl from always being bested by his bigger, stronger brother. When finally Kent has had enough, he lashes out and gets in trouble for fighting. And between outright punches, the endless verbal barbs can keep the battlefield on high alert well into the wee hours.

Lately, you've begun to wonder: *Is family peace even possible?*

Why Do They Fight?

Siblings, obviously, are together a lot. They share parents, space, and belongings. Proverbs 17:17 says, "A friend is always loyal, and a brother is born to help in time of need" (NLT). But because they don't worry about losing a sibling like they would losing a friend, it's easy for them to become careless in their treatment of each other.[1] Other common reasons for sibling strife are:

- The need to feel loved, secure, and significant
- Competition for parents' attention and approval
- A prideful desire always to be right
- Not wanting to share
- An unrealistic quest for fairness
- An older child's desire to be in charge
- A younger child's dislike of being bossed around
- An older child's resentment of being saddled with caring for younger siblings
- Violation of each other's boundaries
- A younger child's jealousy over older siblings having more freedom and a different set of age-based rules
- An older child's resentment over younger children receiving hard-won privileges that the older sibling was denied at the same age
- Hunger, tiredness, or irritability
- The universal desire for a child to want a toy most when someone else—especially a sibling—also wants it[2]

In sibling rivalry, *envy* is the toxic poison that hampers relationships. In fact, the Bible says, "Envy rots the bones" (Prov. 14:30 NIV).

Sibling strife is not uncommon. But when handled effectively, there is hope for true healing as your children mature.

What Could You Do?

Children long to come home to a place where they are treasured as individuals and are treated with kindness and respect by each family member. Here are ways to use boundaries to create this type of home environment.

- Never favor one child over another (see James 2:1) or compare your children to one another. Instead, recognize and praise the unique strengths of each child.
- Don't allow your children to call each other unkind names. Fun nicknames (like *Sunshine*) are permissible but nothing that is hurtful (like *Dummy*).

- Teach children when and what to share. For example, some toys are for all the siblings to share—community toys—while others belong to just one child exclusively.
  - For community toys, teach your child to say, "May I please play with that when you're finished?" Then encourage her to choose another toy and wait for her turn.
  - Don't allow your child to demand that a sibling instantly surrender a community toy. But don't allow a child with a community toy to monopolize it day after day.
- Require your child to ask before playing with an item that belongs to a sibling exclusively.
  - If the sibling has a legitimate reason for not sharing a toy (e.g., baby brother would likely destroy an older sibling's fragile doll), then affirm the older child's legitimate boundary and redirect the younger child.
  - If a legitimate reason doesn't exist, encourage (but don't force) the toy's exclusive owner to share, explaining that doing so would please God. Even so, sharing should be from the heart, not because you demand it. "They are to do good, to be rich in good works, to be generous and ready to share" (1 Tim. 6:18).
- When children come to you with opposing stories, instruct them to sit on opposite ends of the couch and talk together until they can give you an agreed-upon account. This saves everyone time and encourages honesty, communication, and personal responsibility.
- Siblings don't have to agree, but they should be required to speak their opinions respectfully. "Let your speech always be gracious, seasoned with salt, so that you may know how you ought to answer each person" (Col. 4:6).
- If a disagreement gets intense, separate the children. Instruct them to remain in different areas until they're ready to apologize and get along. "Finally, all of you, be like-minded, be sympathetic, love one another, be compassionate and humble" (1 Pet. 3:8 NIV).

- For children who perpetually fight, assign a task for them to complete together. Working together is a positive use of their energy and provides a sense of shared accomplishment. For instance, they can rake leaves, clean the kitchen, sweep the basement, or weed the flowerbed together.
- Make hitting, pinching, and other ways of physically hurting others off-limits in your home. These are serious offenses that call for strong repercussions. The Bible says, "Give up your violence and oppression and do what is just and right" (Ezek. 45:9 NIV). Insist that children keep their hands to themselves unless they are touching a sibling in kindness—and the touch is welcomed.
- Foster the idea of treating family members as well as you would guests. For example, instead of saving the nice dinnerware for visitors only, use it occasionally for the ones you love the most—your immediate family. Exemplify and teach the principle that we give our best for each other.
- Give your children a short list of simple house rules and post them as a reminder. (See "House Rules" on p. 31 for an example.)
- Competition between siblings decreases when each of their emotional tanks is regularly filled with uninterrupted time with a parent. Therefore:
  - Give each child an evening of your time weekly or monthly—a special night just for the two of you.
  - Focus on and talk to each child *individually* throughout the week—when you check homework, read aloud, play a game, pack a school lunch, etc.
- Journal or draw with each child. Encourage them to write or draw whatever is on their minds and place the journal next to your bed. Write back and return the journal to your child's bedside. Don't make spelling and grammar an issue. Some days the book will lay forgotten. Other days, it will allow your child to jot down an observation or pour out her heart in a way she couldn't do verbally.
- Set up fun, collaborative activities that help siblings bond and create happy memories.

- Embark on a continual treasure hunt to mine the unique characteristics, preferences, and bent of each child. Allow your children to be different and help them appreciate both the ways they are alike and distinct from their siblings.
- Don't always ask older siblings to care for younger siblings. If you need childcare help, occasionally assign household jobs to older siblings while you tend to the younger ones.
  - Don't give older children childcare responsibility before they're mature enough to handle it.
  - Factor any additional housework or childcare into your older children's chores to avoid burdening them with too much responsibility.

What Could You Say?

Hold a family meeting, allowing plenty of time for interaction. Begin by saying, "A peaceful home is important to all of us. It's what God wants for us too. The Bible says, 'Do all that you can to live in peace with everyone' (Rom. 12:18 NLT).

"As a family, we've made a lot of great memories together. But lately, the number of fights between you is increasing. When you hit or call each other hurtful names, that saddens God's heart . . . and my heart. I understand that sometimes it's not easy to get along. But instead of using hurtful hands and words, let's find ways to have harmony in our home. I'd like to hear your ideas." [Listen and discuss.]

"If you choose to use hurtful words and actions, you'll also be choosing to do more work around the house together, so you can learn to work well with each other. For every hurtful word spoken, you'll speak a kind word and give a hug for every hurtful action. We will cut back on family outings because it's not fun to go places when the two of you don't get along.

"Sometimes you have happy times together. That pleases the Lord . . . and me. I want you to enjoy that kind of friendship more often. Let's go over our House Rules again." [Have a copy on hand.]

"I've heard you say that I don't treat you fairly because, at times, I treat you *differently*. I love you both with all my heart. My goal isn't to treat each of you exactly the same because you are not the same. You are unique. I decide how to treat you according to what you need, who you are, and how ready you are for something new.

"The Bible says, 'Let each of you look not only to his own interests, but also to the interests of others' (Phil. 2:4). Let's all memorize this verse and talk about how it applies in our home.

"I want our family to please God, encourage each other, and have fun. I know you do too—and I know you *can*. I'm looking forward to more family harmony . . . and having more family fun with both of you!"

Wisdom from God's Word

The Bible presents a profound caution that must be taken seriously: "Whoever says he is in the light and hates his brother is still in darkness. Whoever loves his brother abides in the light, and in him there is no cause for stumbling. But whoever hates his brother is in the darkness and walks in the darkness, and does not know where he is going, because the darkness has blinded his eyes" (1 John 2:9–11).

But the Bible also presents great hope for healing nurturing relationships when believers behave "with all humility and gentleness, with patience, bearing with one another in love, eager to maintain the unity of the Spirit in the bond of peace" (Eph. 4:2–3). After all, what better place than the family to nurture these wonderful virtues?

See these related chapters:
Chapter 6: "Anger and Aggression," page 61
Chapter 10: "Bullying," page 79
Chapter 17: "Disrespectfulness," page 117
Chapter 40: "Temper Tantrums," page 234

36

Sportsmanship Spats

Carter is a natural athlete—he was practically born with a baseball in his hand. Always one of the first kids chosen for teams, he learns new skills with uncanny speed and rarely makes the same mistake twice. But the coach recently told you that if there's one more incident of poor sportsmanship, he'll bench your son for the rest of the season.

When Carter disagrees with an umpire's call, he becomes an equal-opportunity ogre—bad-mouthing competitors, coaches, and officials. And if his team loses a game, Carter's attitude gets ugly . . . fast.

How did winning and being infallible become your pint-sized player's top priority? And how can you help him graciously accept adversity? After all, it's only a game.

What Could You Do?

Famed football coach Vince Lombardi popularized the saying, "Winning isn't everything, it's the only thing." That attitude may have helped make the Green Bay Packers' coach a gridiron legend, but it won't help your child become a good sport.[1] For that, you could:

- Consider your own example. How do *you* behave when you disagree with an official's call or when your child doesn't get to play the position you think he's best-suited for or when he's overlooked for advancement? You don't have to pretend that winning isn't fun, and you don't have to agree with a coach's or official's every decision. But you *do* need to model good parental sportsmanship.

- Teach your child to focus on the joy and privilege of *participation*, cultivate humility and teamwork, handle wins and losses with dignity, be disciplined and stick with tough tasks, tackle new challenges, and push toward his personal best.
- Praise your child's effort and positive attitude, not just his ability. Effort and attitude are both within his control. Often, ability is not. Controlling the amount of effort expended helps a child grasp the cause-and-effect relationship between effort and progress. The same is true of controlling his attitude. It also helps him see himself as an active agent in his own success.[2] But a child who is hooked on results-based praise believes he has to win at all costs, fears losing, and can be less likely to take chances.[3]
  - When watching sporting events, compliment the efforts and good attitudes of those who perform well and display sportsmanlike conduct even if they don't always win.
- Help your child explore Scriptures related to pride and humility. For example: "God opposes the proud but gives grace to the humble" (1 Pet. 5:5).
- Point out athletes who display good sportsmanship. Watch movies and read books about godly athletes, such as Eric Liddell in *Chariots of Fire*.
- Role-play how to reflect Christlike character in the face of both favorable and unfavorable decisions—and wins and losses.
- If you always "lose on purpose" when playing games with your child—even just to help him experience the joy of victory—stop! Allowing a poor sport to lose will help him face reality—in truth, no one wins all the time. Humility will help him replace bad habits with good ones in a safe, supportive environment.
- Frame poor sportsmanship as your *child's* problem to solve. Tell him he has a choice: He can choose unsportsmanlike con-

duct and forego recreational activities for a defined time, or he can choose good sportsmanship along with the reward—and privilege—of continued participation.

What Could You Say?

To your son, who may soon be sidelined because of poor sportsmanship, you could say, "What a game! You have as much hustle as anyone on your team—maybe more.

"But I noticed something that's drawing attention away from your game. And that's your attitude. Your coach says you'll be sidelined for the rest of the season if you continue choosing to be a poor sport. I'd like to hear your thoughts. What's going on, son?" [Listen carefully.]

"Tell me what good sportsmanship means to you." [Listen, then supplement with your own brief definition and description.]

"You were born with good athletic ability. That's a gift from God. But the times you kept trying when others had given up, when you graciously accepted a call you didn't like, and when you acted maturely after a loss, these things matter more than winning—to God and to me. I hope they'll always matter more to you too.

"God's Word says, 'Let every person be subject to the governing authorities. For there is no authority except from God, and those that exist have been instituted by God' (Rom. 13:1). When you're on that field, the umpire is your authority.

"There'll be times you disagree with him. If your coach disagrees, too, it's his job to talk to the ump. It's your job to accept the decision and focus on playing the game. I know that's hard and sometimes it can seem unfair. But God knows what's happening. He sees. And his Word tells us he'll cause *all things* to work together for our good when we're committed to him (Rom. 8:28). That includes bad calls and lost games.

"Whether you win or lose, what matters most is that you honor God, encourage your teammates, and enjoy the game. That means you obey the rules, don't hurt anyone on purpose, help your teammates succeed, be respectful, try your best, learn from mistakes, and accept the win or loss with grace. Let's talk about each one of these. Tell me about a time when you acted this way, and how it made you feel." [Draw your child out on various aspects of sportsmanship.]

"You have a choice. You can be a good sport and enjoy the privilege of playing on the team. Or you can be a poor sport and sit on the bench. I've seen you be a good sport, and I know you can do it. I'm on your team, and I'll be cheering for you. When you put forth your best effort with a good attitude, you're always a champ—whether you win or lose the game."

Wisdom from God's Word

The Bible says, "Pride goes before destruction, and a haughty spirit before a fall" (Prov. 16:18). It takes great sacrifice and discipline to run the good race in this life and to do so with a Christlike attitude. Only those who learn to exercise self-control will be rewarded. Aim your child toward the eternal prize described in 1 Corinthians 9:25–27: "Every athlete exercises self-control in all things. They do it to receive a perishable wreath, but we an imperishable. So I do not run aimlessly; I do not box as one beating the air. But I discipline my body and keep it under control."

See these related chapters:

37

Stealing

"May I have a candy bar please?"

Pushing the shopping cart, you glance at your list and then check the time. It's too close to dinner for your son, Caleb, to eat candy.

"Not now, sweetie."

"But I'm *really hungry*," Caleb complains.

"You may pick out an apple to eat on the ride home."

"Okay," comes the disappointed reply.

After checking out, you hand Caleb the apple. But as you exit the store an employee approaches and says, "Ma'am, I believe your son has something that wasn't paid for."

Looking back, you see Caleb—wide-eyed and frozen in his tracks.

Slowly, he reaches under his shirttail and pulls two giant candy bars from his back pocket. Now it's your move. . . .

What Could You Do?

At its core, stealing is the decision to choose your wants over the rights and needs of another. Sometimes people steal out of desperation. But typically, stealing is a clear instance of selfish desire, greed, and covetousness.

So how do you train your child not to steal? In the case of your son, who pilfered two candy bars:

- Resist the temptation to respond out of your own embarrassment or to rescue your child from the embarrassment and natural consequences of getting caught stealing. Be thankful that his behavior was revealed so you can deal with it. Pray that the guilt and embarrassment will serve as a lifelong deterrent to stealing.
- Require your son to return what he stole, confess his wrong act to the store manager (making eye contact), apologize, and ask for forgiveness.
- Together with your child, memorize Exodus 20:15: "You shall not steal."
- Even though he returned the stolen merchandise, require your son to pay back double the amount stolen—a principle from Exodus 22:4–9. If he doesn't have the funds, work out a repayment plan and require him to earn the money in an age-appropriate way.
  - For example, a young child could do household chores.
  - Older ones could rake the neighbor's leaves, mow lawns, wash cars, walk dogs, etc. Ephesians 4:28 gives this counsel: "Anyone who has been stealing must steal no longer, but must work, doing something useful with their own hands" (NIV).

What Could You Say?

"I love it when we both go shopping together. But what you did today was wrong and must never happen again.

"Taking things that you don't pay for or things that belong to someone else is stealing. Stealing displeases God, and it displeases me.

"How would *you* feel if your brother stole your favorite toy?" [Wait for a candid response.]

"God tells us in Scripture: 'You shall not steal' (Deut. 5:19; Ex. 20:15). Stealing is also against the law. People can go to jail for stealing. When you choose to take something that doesn't belong to you, you disobey God's Word *and* break the law.

"When you chose to steal the candy bars, you also chose to not eat any candy for a week. Even though you've apologized to the store manager, asked him to forgive you, and paid back the amount that four candy bars cost, the Bible says 'A good name is to be chosen rather than great riches' (Prov. 22:1). Why do you think that is?" [Discuss the importance of a person's reputation.] "This is your chance to win back the trust of the people at the grocery store—and to win my trust in you and your trust in yourself.

"This doesn't mean you'll never again be *tempted* to steal. It's not wrong to be tempted. But it is wrong to *act* on the temptation. God says he'll never let us face a temptation that he won't give us the power to resist (Heb. 2:18; 4:15). That's a promise.

"I love you, and I know you can choose to do the right thing. Would you be willing to decide in your heart to be honest?" [Wait for a response.] "Isn't God good to allow us to learn from our lessons and move on, knowing we're forgiven?"

Wisdom from God's Word

Through our relationship with Christ, God empowers us to live a life that is right in his sight. When we do, we receive the richest gain of all—God's fellowship and favor. "Ill-gotten treasures are of no value, but righteousness delivers from death" (Prov. 10:2). We have a choice to make. Jesus put it this way: "One who is faithful in a very little is also faithful in much, and one who is dishonest in a very little is also dishonest in much" (Luke 16:10).

See these related chapters:
Chapter 24: "Lying," page 152
Chapter 27: "Money and Materialism," page 170

Substance Abuse

Putting away laundry in your ten-year-old daughter Ava's room, you stumble over her backpack. Picking it up, you notice that it's wet on the bottom. You take it to the kitchen, expecting to find a leaking water bottle or spilled soft drink.

But what's that *odor*? It can't be . . . but it is! A near-empty bottle of liquor. How do you handle this serious issue with Ava?

Substance Abuse in Children

The majority of people addicted to potentially harmful substances—including alcohol, tobacco, and illegal and prescription drugs—take their first sniff, snort, puff, or injection as a preteen. Before age thirteen, nearly one out of four children has had their first drink. Some three million twelve-year-olds have tried an illicit drug, and one out of ten has used marijuana.[1]

While some use *illegal* drugs, most children abuse substances found in their own homes. A parent's alcohol, megavitamins, over-the-counter medicines, and prescription drugs—plus solvents, aerosols, and household glues—are common choices.

Through chemical substances, children experience exhilaration, decreased inhibitions, peer acceptance, independence from family standards, and a temporary escape from everyday pressures. Whether sampling leads to addiction depends on the individual child's mindset, home environment, genetic makeup, and other factors.

Where Does It Start?

School counselors report that children introduce each other to drug and alcohol-related experimentation as early as fifth grade. Sleepovers can place kids in danger when there is a temptation to show off in front of peers after parents go to bed. Children who regularly come home to an empty house can be vulnerable. Without the maturity to predict outcomes, children cannot comprehend the dangers inherent in their actions or the potential damage to their brains or bodies. In their minds, they are invincible.

Factors that lure children include:

- Appeals from advertisements
- Apathetic attitudes of parents
- Availability in the home
- Natural curiosity
- Peer pressure/seeking acceptance from peers
- An angry, rebellious spirit
- Consuming interest in thrill seeking

What Do You Look For?

What are signs indicating involvement with substance abuse?[2]

Stage 1: Experimentation

- Smell of tobacco or alcohol on breath/clothing
- Change in behavior
- Interest in thrill-seeking activities
- Excessive desire to fit in with a group

Stage 2: Frequent Use

- Change of friends
- Disappearance of things from your home, purse, or cabinets (money, alcohol, jewelry, prescriptions, over-the-counter medications)
- Unexplained absences

- Changes in appearance (dilated pupils, complexion changes, puffiness)
- Deteriorating school performance
- Disrespect
- Dishonesty

Stage 3: Regular Use

- Escalation of conflicts at home and at school
- Reclusive behavior
- Loss of interest in family, school, extracurricular activities, and church events
- Changes in personal appearance and attitude

Stage 4: Addiction

- Inability to get up in the morning
- Headache, stomachache, and weight loss
- Escalation of conflicts with parents and others
- Absence of ambition and motivation
- Disconnection from the family
- Anger, stemming from the stress of the addiction and being questioned about possible use

The Bible says, "Do not envy a man of violence and do not choose any of his ways, for the devious person is an abomination to the Lord, but the upright are in his confidence" (Prov. 3:31–32).

What are items and behaviors that indicate involvement?

- Cigarettes, cigars, tobacco, or marijuana
- Unusual or excessive use of vitamins, energy drinks, or caffeine
- Quickly emptied or missing cold remedy packages
- Missing knives and spoons, repurposed for crushing and sniffing pills
- Empty aerosol cans, paper bags
- Liquor bottles, beer cans, etc.
- Drug paraphernalia, such as pincers, pen cases for snorting, glue bottles, mirrors, or lighters

- Missing medicine bottles/containers
- Missing liquor

What Could You Do?

Some of the strongest safeguards against substance abuse include:

- Good parental role modeling
- A home environment where children feel loved, significant, and secure
- A strong emphasis on prevention, including a healthy respect for the dangers of abuse[3]
- Open lines of communication
- Authentic faith in a loving God—supported by church and Sunday school attendance
- Regular volunteerism to nurture a lifelong habit of serving others

Young children growing up in homes with proper supervision, effective discipline, and clear expectations for behavior often view alcohol misuse as harmful and are reluctant to initiate early substance abuse. In fact, in homes where the parent-child relationship is strong, children are less inclined to use alcohol in their teen years as well.[4]

To emphasize prevention, you could:

- Speak calmly and openly with your child (and her friends) about the importance of staying away from drugs and alcohol.
- Communicate clear rules that your family does not tolerate underage alcohol or drug usage.
- Know her whereabouts after school and be involved with her activities, her friends, and their parents. Visit with the parents. Go to their homes and see where your child will be spending time.
- Assure your daughter that she can come to you if she is ever concerned that a friend is having problems with drugs or alcohol. Tell her you are on her team to help keep her and her peers safe.
- Set the right example. Do you abuse alcohol or drugs? If so, take responsibility for your failures, get help, and prayerfully seek to model right choices.

– Consider barring alcohol from your home as long as your children live there, even if you choose to drink socially elsewhere. However, for many people, the reason they choose not to drink is this Scripture: "It is better not to eat meat or drink wine or do anything else if it might cause another believer to stumble" (Rom. 14:21 NLT).

– If you smoke cigarettes, for your child's sake, quit.

In the case of discovering a bottle of alcohol in your daughter's backpack, immediate intervention is imperative:

• Remove the bottle from the backpack and talk to your daughter as soon as possible. Gather as much information as she is willing to share. For example, was this a onetime occurrence or is it a pattern? If a pattern, when did it start? Were others involved?

• See if there are other items in her room that may indicate additional issues such as drug use or theft.

• Consider your child's behavior over the past few weeks or months. Have there been observable changes? If you suspect (or now realize) that this is not a onetime event, arrange for her to meet with a professional therapist. Likewise, if she actively resists your concerned intervention, seek professional help.

– Be cautious of professionals who prescribe medications as a quick fix for problems rather than helping your child practice new, healthy behaviors that teach discipline and encourage long-lasting change.

• Place medications, alcohol, solvents, glues, and other substances that could be abused under lock and key.

• Drug test your daughter if you suspect drug use.

– If you believe she is manipulating her at-home drug tests, use tests that are sent to a lab to check for adulteration (watering down, drinking liquids that "cleanse" their system, etc.).

• Until you are certain her behavior has changed, eliminate her overnight stays at friends' homes.

• Arrange for her to meet with local police or other experts who explain the ramifications of continued drug and alcohol abuse.

- Arrange for a tour of the local jail to help her visualize and understand the repercussions of breaking the law.
- If other children are complicit with your daughter's alcohol and/ or drug use, explore with their parents how to help all your children stay away from drugs and alcohol.
  - Closely supervise joint activities or, as needed, help your child choose new friends.
  - Resist the temptation to blame other children whom you consider to be bad influences on your child. Other parents may just as readily think that *your* child is a bad influence. (The truth is, your child *is* involved.)
- As often as possible, accompany your daughter to her extracurricular activities and bring her along to yours. She may not like this initially, but remind her that the reason for this action is because she has broken your trust.

What Could You Say?

"Over the years you have earned more and more of my trust, and I've been so proud of you for making right choices. But last night, I found a bottle of alcohol inside your backpack, and I need you to choose to make a good decision right now and tell me the truth. Where did the bottle come from?" [If she is forthcoming, express appreciation, then continue.] "Please help me understand when you began drinking and why you do it." [Allow plenty of time to delve deeply into the "whys" of her poor choice.]

"Giving a child alcohol is against the law. Children who drink alcohol can start a habit they can't stop—an addiction. This is a serious issue, one that can affect your whole life. The Bible says, 'Without counsel plans fail, but with many advisers they succeed' (Prov. 15:22). I believe you can choose to make wise decisions. And to help you, we're going to visit a wise counselor a couple of times a week after school for a while."

If other children were involved, you could say, "When you and your friends choose to break the rules, it tells me it's not wise for you to spend time together. So for the next two months, you won't be seeing them. After that, I'll watch you more closely when you're with them, giving you time to rebuild my trust in you and your trust in yourself and each other.

"There will be no playtime after school for the next two weeks. You're grounded. On Saturday, we're going to watch a video about the effects of misusing alcohol. We're also going to visit a place downtown that helps people stop abusing alcohol.

"When you choose to obey our family's rules, you won't have to worry about getting caught doing wrong things. You'll also be rewarded with more trust . . . and more choices about how you spend your free time and who you spend it with.

"I love you deeply and care about your well-being. Your value is beyond measure. Your choices matter—now and later in your life. I believe God can help you turn this wrong choice into an important learning lesson. Let's pray and ask him to do that."

Wisdom from God's Word

On the issue of substance abuse, the Bible provides clear instruction. Proverbs 20:1 presents a strong warning: "Wine is a mocker and beer a brawler; whoever is led astray by them is not wise."

Fortunately, as believers we can have full assurance that no habit, addiction, or temptation is too much for us to handle with God's help. "Faithful is the one who called you and he will do it" (1 Thess. 5:24).*

See these related chapters:

Chapter 21: "Harmful Habits and Addictions," page 137
Chapter 24: "Lying," page 152
Chapter 30: "Peer Pressure," page 186

---

* For more information on drugs, see the U.S. Drug Enforcement Administration's Drug Fact Sheets, available at http://www.dea.gov/druginfo/factsheets.shtml/ and the National Institute on Drug Abuse's Commonly Abused Drugs Charts, available at http://www.drugabuse.gov/drugs-abuse /commonly-abused-drugs-charts.

39

Tardiness

You're not a morning person—you may rise, but you sure don't shine. Fortunately, God blessed you with two children who get up and get themselves ready. But the third—well, Payton is worse than *you* in the morning. While her siblings are like microwaves, your "Crock-Pot child" lies in bed and spends twenty minutes surveying the pattern on the wallpaper. Her slow gear keeps you running back upstairs throughout the morning, making sure she'll be ready to leave the house on time. It's not exactly the aerobics program you had in mind.

What's more, you're late almost every day—late leaving the house, late getting the kids to school (where you must sign tardy notes), and late to work when traffic slows. This stressful beginning often dampens the rest of your day.

"Payton even came into the world two weeks late," you muse. "I should have seen this coming!"

What Could You Do?

- To help your slow starter develop timely habits, first make sure she gets adequate sleep. Children require significant blocks of deep sleep to support their developing minds and bodies. While some children require more sleep than others, here are general guidelines.[1]

Age	Estimated hours of sleep needed daily
1–3	12–14 (including naps)
4–6	10–12
7–12	10–11
13–18	8–9

- As a parent, model punctuality. Expect your child to do as you *do,* not just as you *say.*
- One to two hours prior to bedtime, turn off all media. TV, movies, and computers stimulate the brain, making it harder for children to fall asleep. Set the stage for satisfying rest by using the time just before bed to bathe, read, pray, and do other relaxing activities.
- Balance blood sugar with a bedtime snack that includes protein, fat, and carbohydrates. This could be half a tuna sandwich, peanut butter on a banana, or almonds and apples (subject to any food sensitivities she may have).
- Have your child place her schoolbooks, gym clothes, and other necessities for the next day in her backpack by the door, ready to grab and go in the morning.
- Lay out the next day's clothing the night before.
- To encourage a child who procrastinates at bedtime, see chapter 8 "Bedtime Battles," p. 71.
- Even with plenty of rest, some children are slower to greet the morning. Let your child choose an alarm clock and help her get into the habit of setting it to ring in plenty of time to accomplish her morning routine.
- Train your child to be fully dressed *before* leaving her room in the morning.
- For the visual learner, make a colorful chart listing the steps to getting ready for school.
- Make a recording telling your child exactly what to do from the time she opens her eyes until she leaves the house. The cheerful prompts in your own voice will help her and allow you to get yourself and the rest of the family ready too. For example, at

6:30, you could enter the room and press "play." Your child would hear your voice say, "Good morning, Sunshine! Time to get up. It's going to be a great day." For the next ten minutes, favorite songs help her wake up. Then your voice says, "All right, honey, wiggle those toes and stretch." Recorded prompts then guide her through making her bed, brushing her teeth and hair, dressing, and coming to breakfast. Between instructions, you could add reminders like, "Almost time to come down to breakfast. I love you and can't wait to see your smile this morning!"

- Keep several recordings on hand, each timed to different schedule requirements, with routines appropriate for that particular day (such as getting ready for church).
- When your child is able to be on time without the recordings, celebrate and recognize her progress.

• Enlist your child's thoughts on how to solve her tardiness problem. Kids need practice solving the problems they create.
• Chronic distractibility and inability to get ready on time may indicate an underlying issue, such as ADHD. Your child's doctor can help you evaluate screening options.

What Could You Say?

In the case of your daughter, who's continually late for school, you could say, "Honey, I understand that getting up on time is hard. It's hard for me, too. It's your job to get yourself ready on time. When you don't, it causes tension and we start the day playing catch-up. The Bible says that 'there is a time for every matter under heaven' (Eccles. 3:1), and that includes a time to leave home in the morning.

"For now, this is the new plan: I'll make a recording that helps you wake up and get ready. You'll hear my voice saying what to do next. There will be music, too, so let's pick the songs you want to hear each morning.

"I'd also like to hear your thoughts for solving this problem." [Listen and comment.]

"I want to encourage you to choose to get ready on time, so for every minute you choose to be late leaving in the morning, you'll go to bed the same number of minutes earlier that night. For example, if you're ready to leave at 7:45 instead of 7:30 tomorrow, you'll go to bed at 8:45 instead of 9:00 tomorrow night. After you choose to get ready on time for a full week, you will get a reward, like doing a fun craft together!

"I'm *for you* 100 percent. I know you can get ready and leave on time. It will be a joy to see your progress and to celebrate it as a family. And I know your teachers will be happy too!"

Wisdom from God's Word

Training children to organize and prepare for the future starts with each new tomorrow. When we get ready on time, we honor God who put everything in order, we honor others, and we honor ourselves. "Everything should be done in a fitting and orderly way" (1 Cor. 14:40 NIV).

See these related chapters:
Chapter 8: "Bedtime Battles," page 71
Chapter 31: "Procrastination," page 191

40

Temper Tantrums

The very thought of grocery shopping with your twin toddlers, Isabella and Ian, fills you with dread. You try to sneak out to the store on weekends while someone else sits with the kids during naptime. But inevitably a run to the store is necessary during the week.

At these times you just hope Isabella doesn't fall to the ground, as she's done in the past, kicking and screaming in the cereal aisle. That last tantrum lasted several minutes—though it felt like an eternity. And then, just as Isabella was calming down, Ian pitched a jar of mayonnaise out of the cart.

Things must change! But how can grocery shopping be enjoyable with Isabella and Ian in tow?

What Could You Do?

The secret to discipline during temper tantrums is found in one word: *detachment*. The art of doing much by appearing to do little, detachment has the power to control tantrums and put an end to embarrassing public spectacles. It's an extremely effective boundary to build with younger children. The key, however, is being detached from your child's *actions* but not from your *child*. Understanding the difference is essential to mastering this technique.

Imagine you're at the grocery store and your daughter puts a box of cereal in your cart. You take it away, and she begins to howl. Here's how to detach:

- Place her in the seat of the cart if she's not already there.
- Cup her face with your hands so she's looking you in the eyes.
- In a calm, deliberate manner say, "We do not behave this way in the store. If you continue to scream, we'll go straight to the car."
- Remember: You're trying to win an award for the Best Detached Parent performance. When kids are out of control, cool them down by being firm, focused, calm, and authoritative. Then go back to your shopping immediately, detached from your child's behavior, not allowing her tantrum to dominate the shopping experience.
- If she continues screaming, you must do the hard thing—leave your groceries in the store and take her and her brother to the car. You might ask an employee to hold your items until you can return for them later. The most important matter is training your child during this teachable moment.
- While inconvenient, the boundary you build now will help change your child's behavior. Typically, a few instances of receiving the repercussion by leaving the store will be sufficient.
- Inconsistency or conceding is an open invitation for your child to act up again. Firmly reinforced boundaries will get the results you desire.
- Occasionally, you may choose to give your child a small, special reward for good behavior on a shopping trip. However, a special treat should not be expected or given every time. A simple "Thank you for being my happy helper!" can go a long way in affirming positive behavior.
- Before future trips to the grocery store, feed your child. Also, have realistic expectations for how much shopping your child can be expected to do cheerfully.

What Could You Say?

When you first arrive at the store, while still in the car, you could say to your child, "We're going shopping together and you'll ride in the cart. You can be my happy helper. You may pick out the fruit for our snack today and help me choose vegetables. When we get home, you can help put things away, and then we'll have our snack. Let's go!"

As you shop, expect your child to express a desire for things that aren't on your list. You want to encourage questions and conversation, balanced with respect for your final decision. You can say, "Not today, but thank you for asking."

If your child acts out and you practice detachment but the tantrum continues, calmly state, "You're choosing to go to the car. I'll finish shopping another time." Park the cart, remove your child, and calmly walk her to the car, ignoring all protests—regardless of how robust—along the way.

In the car, repeat your plan. "When you choose to stop crying, we can go back into the store and finish shopping. You can be my helper." If your child is compliant, return to the store and retrieve your cart.

Be willing to sit in the car for a while. Investing the time now teaches your child that you're serious about what you've said and reduces the chances of a repeat performance. If the crying continues after sitting in the car for several minutes, drive home.

Remember, you never detach from your child, you simply detach from the behavior. The beauty of detachment is you don't say much. Calm, authoritative control is key. For some parents, this is quite difficult. When you become upset, your voice gets louder and may rise in pitch. To lower it, imagine your pitch as descending steps on a flight of stairs. Lower it one step at a time, ending on a soft, low note. Definitely not a whisper, but a gentle, firm word spoken with your eyes locked on hers. You win the battle by *not reacting* but by remaining calm and in control.

Wisdom from God's Word

Proverbs 25:28 says, "A man without self-control is like a city broken into and left without walls." Tantrums reveal an immature and defiant heart, which, left untended, is likely to grow more rebellious with each passing year. The process that moves a child's heart from disrespect to obedience does not happen overnight. But with love, perseverance, and patience, you can guide your child to handle her emotions properly. When you do, the rewards will last a lifetime.

See these related chapters:
Chapter 6: "Anger and Aggression," page 61
Chapter 7: "Back Talk," page 67
Chapter 17: "Disrespectfulness," page 117
Chapter 32: "Profanity and Name-Calling," page 196

41

Whining

Clearly your son, Adam, is having a great time at the birthday party . . . but now it's time to leave. You suspect your announcement may not be well received. And you're right.

"Nooo! Don't make me gooo!" With each word, Adam's whiny voice grows louder and higher. Soon others start to stare as the drama unfolds.

"Adam," you begin, "that's enough."

"But I don't waaaant to go," he persists.

"You quiet down, young man, and listen to me."

"Pleaseeee! I want to staaaay!"

Adam's lament sounds like a sad song on a country music radio station. But you can't find the on/off switch.

Why Do Children Whine?

Whining is manipulative, emotional resistance, calculated to weaken your resolve, reverse your decision, and undermine your authority. Often accompanied by its first cousin—begging—whining works effectively only when you permit it to work. Those who allow their children to whine train them to believe that with enough moaning and groaning any parental decision can be reversed.

Begin early to teach your child to communicate wants and needs in a healthy way and to accept your wise, loving authority.

What Could You Do?

- Speak confidently, gently, and respectfully to your child. This sets the example to imitate when speaking to you and others.
- Don't give in to whining. Calmly and firmly tell your child to use words and a normal tone of voice to communicate.
- Whenever possible, answer when your child speaks to you. A parent who regularly ignores a child can unintentionally encourage whining in order to be heard.
- Sometimes, simply redirecting your child can interrupt the "whine cycle" as you purposefully focus attention *away* from what you're directing your child to give up and *toward* something new or different that lies ahead. For example, when your child begs to stay up late on a school night, firmly reinforce the rule, but redirect by asking what story you should read together *now*. Remind him that late bedtimes occur only on special occasions.
- Pay attention to your child's daily routines and activities. A child who's overly hungry or tired, for example, may be more prone to whining. That doesn't mean you must tolerate whining, but it may help you address the root cause for whiny behavior.

In the case of your son, who whined when you announced it was time to leave the birthday party, you could also:

- Review behavioral expectations with your child *before* arriving at the party.
- Give him advance notice that you'll be leaving in ten minutes. Remind him again five minutes before departure time. Knowing what will happen next can help a child transition.
- If he calms down, changes his attitude, and asks respectfully for what he wants, you may occasionally decide to reward his compliant efforts by attempting to find a win-win compromise. Perhaps you agree to stay at the party for five more minutes to reinforce that "good things happen when you use your words and normal voice to make a reasonable request."[1] But don't feel pressured to change your plans just because your child asks nicely.

What Could You Say?

Retreat to a private area if possible and look at your child eye-to-eye—with him sitting on your lap or you kneeling at his level. Then you could say, "What you want is important to me. But I will *not* respond to whining. The Bible says, 'Do everything without grumbling or arguing' (Phil. 2:14 NIV). Choosing to use your normal voice helps me focus on what you're asking. It doesn't get drowned out by your whining.

"Sometimes my answer to what you want will be *yes*. Sometimes it'll be *no*. But when you choose to whine, it will always be *no*.

"If you choose to continue whining right now, we're still leaving. But instead of going to [name an upcoming activity your child is looking forward to], you'll stay home. You'll either choose not to whine when it's time to leave or stay home next time there's a fun place to go.

"What am I saying will happen if you choose to continue whining?" [Let him repeat back to you what he heard to ensure he understands.] "That's right.

"What you have to say is important to me. As soon as you use your normal voice, I'll be ready to listen."

Wisdom from God's Word

God invites us to talk to him continually through prayer. He assures us that he's listening and promises to meet all our needs "according to the riches of his glory in Christ Jesus" (Phil. 4:19 NIV). Additionally, Scripture provides clear instruction about *how* to ask. "Do not be anxious about anything, but in everything by prayer and supplication with thanksgiving let your requests be made known to God. And the peace of God, which surpasses all understanding, will guard your hearts and your minds in Christ Jesus" (Phil. 4:6).

When you teach your child to communicate effectively, you establish a foundation that will help him experience warm fellowship with the Creator and those created in his image. Philippians 2:14–15 says, "Do everything without grumbling or arguing, so that you may become blameless and pure, 'children of God without fault in a warped and crooked generation.' Then you will shine among them like stars in the sky" (NIV).

See these related chapters:
Chapter 6: "Anger and Aggression," page 61
Chapter 17: "Disrespectfulness," page 117
Chapter 40: "Temper Tantrums," page 234

Epilogue

What If This Letter Were
Written to You?

Have you ever found yourself lying awake late at night, asking . . .

Am I really doing the right thing—really?
Am I being too harsh or hard . . . too lax or lenient?
Will all this painful work of parenting ever pay off?
Will my children value the years of teaching and training?
Will the kids grasp their need for being confronted over curfews?
Will they see why we had to have battles over boundaries?
Will their character ever resemble the character of Christ?

I doubt there is any parent who *hasn't* wrestled with these same questions at one time or another.

During their son's early childhood years, Allison and Aaron were permissive parents. Then when Jared turned ten, the couple realized that godly boundaries—complete with rewards and repercussions—were no longer an option—but an absolute necessity! However, building boundaries where none existed became doubly difficult. Yet this couple persisted, remaining committed, clear, and consistent as they worked with Jared, day by day, month by month, year after year.

"Eventually," says Allison, "Jared learned to respect both the boundaries we set *and* us as parents." And so it was . . . after Jared grew up and left home, Allison and Aaron received a letter written in Jared's own hand.

Dear Mom and Dad,

First, I want to thank you for everything you've done for me and all the love you've shown me through the years. I know I wasn't the "easiest" kid, but thanks to all of your love and support, I think I'm turning out all right.

I really appreciate your patience and acceptance of me, especially through some low points in my life. Your love is what helped me get through it. And I'm becoming the man you always said I could be. All the groundings . . . and spankings . . . and talks we had have put things into focus for me. (You and I both know I tend to learn things the hard way.) But they all were for a reason. I really see that now.

It's because of your hard work that I know I will be the best man I can be in life, in love, and with God. I thank him for parents who gave me so much when I didn't deserve it. You gave me a shoulder to cry on, put a roof over my head, and kept a watchful eye on my life. Oh, and let's not forget how much you've had to spend on me over the past twenty-two years!

Dad, thank you for spending so much time with me in my youth. I will never forget our hunting and fishing trips and all the wisdom you shared with me around the campfire. I will always look back on those days as some of the best times of my life. I want to make you proud, to provide the kind of support to my future family that you did for ours, and to put the values you taught me to good use. You never gave up on me . . . no matter how hard I made it on you. Who I am today is because of your love and guidance.

Mom, thank you for always being so understanding of my special needs. You cared about me when no one else in this world seemed to. You never turned your back on me. And though I don't deserve the love you've always shown me, I want you to know it's meant the world to me. Your patience, the talks and guidance you gave me, taught me how to respect a woman.

Your heart is so big, if the girl God's chosen for me to marry is half the person you are, that would be amazing! I only hope that someday I can put the values you taught me into practice with my own children so they cherish them as much as I will the rest of my life.

My biggest fear has always been that I might let you down. But I won't let that happen. I love you both.

Your loving and forever grateful son,

Jared

Implementing godly parenting principles doesn't *guarantee* that your children will one day "rise up and call you blessed" (Prov. 31:28). But it does greatly increase your chances beyond what they'd be if you let your children follow their own undisciplined way.

As a parent, your heart, prayers, and hope (complete with your blood, sweat, and tears) are to be focused on the highest purpose of all—to do what is truly in the best interest of your child.

But what is best? What does "best" mean? The views of people widely vary.

Instead of polling the populous for their opinions (money, education, profession, family, inheritance)—there is only one opinion that matters: What does God say is best? What has our heavenly Father said?

Realize, he has already communicated what his highest and best purpose is for us: "My prayer for you is that you may have still more love—a love that is full of knowledge and wise insight. I want you to be able always to recognize the highest and the best, and to live sincere and blameless lives until the day of Jesus Christ. I want to see your lives full of true goodness, produced by the power that Jesus Christ gives you to the praise and glory of God" (Phil. 1:9–11 PHILLIPS).

The Bible says in Romans 8:29 that we are "predestined to be conformed to the image of his Son." Yes, that is what's best . . . being conformed to the character of Christ.

As you pursue this highest and best purpose, my heart's desire is that these words (which were said about Jesus), could one day be said about *your* child . . .

"The child grew and became strong,
filled with wisdom.
And the favor of God was upon him."

(Luke 2:40)

How to Lead Your
Child to Christ

"Son, you are too young," says a mother to her guilt-ridden twelve-year-old son grappling with sin and desperately seeking a remedy for the unrest reverberating through his spirit.[1] He hopes his mother can point him to God for peace. But peace is unnecessarily postponed. And Jesse Irvin Overholtzer doesn't hear a clear gospel presentation until he's a twenty-year-old college student. By then he's more than ready to respond.

Jesse's childhood experience, coupled with a famous theologian's premise that a child at the age of five can truly commit to saving faith, moved him to establish Child Evangelism Fellowship (CEF), a mission organization committed to evangelizing and discipling children all over the world. In 2007, CEF reached more than eight million children in over 158 countries.

Jesse's heart reflects the heart Jesus clearly conveys in Mark 10:14: "Let the children come to me; do not hinder them, for to such belongs the kingdom of God." History reveals that many of those "little children" have grown up to become giants of the faith.

Can Your Child Really Understand Salvation?
Some people say you should wait to talk with children about spiritual issues until they can think abstractly. Yet parents who wait are

often dismayed as their children grow up with no spiritual roots because the seeds of truth weren't planted in their hearts from infancy on. Proverbs 22:6 offers these words of instruction to parents: "Train up a child in the way he should go; even when he is old he will not depart from it."

God created us with the capacity and desire to relate to him. He alone has a direct gateway into the human heart, bypassing our senses and speaking directly to the spirit. He draws us to himself and makes us ready to respond to the offer of salvation—regardless of age. In Matthew 18:3, Jesus said: "Truly I tell you, unless you change and become like little children, you will never enter the kingdom of heaven." Is it any wonder that children are often the most quick to respond to the "good news" that Jesus came to save us?

How to Present God's Plan of Salvation to Your Child

When your child asks questions about how to receive Jesus as Lord and Savior, are you prepared to present God's plan of salvation? Here is a simple script that can help you share God's amazing plan of salvation:

God

Say: "God created everything in the world, including you. He loves you and will always love you."

"In the beginning God created the heavens and the earth" (Gen. 1:1 NLT).

Say: "God created a perfect world. But he let Adam and Eve have choices. They chose to disobey God and do wrong things. We do the same. Sometimes we are selfish, hurt others, and even forget about God."

"Therefore, just as sin came into the world through one man, and death through sin, and so death spread to all men because all sinned" (Rom. 5:12).

Sin

Say: "This creates a problem between us and God. It's called sin. Sin is knowing what is right but choosing what is wrong."

"So whoever knows the right thing to do and fails to do it, for him it is sin" (James 4:17).

The Penalty of Sin

Say: "Sin creates a lot of sadness in the world. It also does something sad in our relationship with God—it makes him seem far away."

"Your iniquities have made a separation between you and your God, and your sins have hidden his face from you so that he does not hear" (Isa. 59:2).

Say: "Because God is only good, all our sins could keep us separated from God forever—even after we die. But listen to this: God never stopped loving Adam and Eve even when they did wrong. And he never stops loving you and me either—no matter what!"

"I have loved you with an everlasting love; I have drawn you with unfailing kindness" (Jer. 31:3 NIV).

The Price of Sin

Say: "Because God loves us so much, he thought of a way to save us from the sad results of sin. God made a way to personally pay the penalty for sin by sending his Son Jesus to die on the cross for you and me. We should be punished for what we've done wrong, but Jesus took our punishment instead."

"For God so loved the world, that he gave his only Son, that whoever believes in him should not perish but have eternal life" (John 3:16).

"But God shows his love for us in that while we were still sinners, Christ died for us" (Rom. 5:8).

Forgiveness

Say: "Because Jesus did this, all the wrong things you've ever done can be forgiven. And if you believe this, you will be saved from your sins. God is just waiting for you to ask."

"Believe in the Lord Jesus, and you will be saved" (Acts 16:31).

"If you confess with your mouth that Jesus is Lord and believe in your heart that God raised him from the dead, you will be saved" (Rom. 10:9).

Say: "When we tell God that we believe Jesus died for us, and then ask him to forgive our sins, he forgives us right away. He makes our hearts clean so he sees no trace of sin there."

"If we confess our sins, he is faithful and just to forgive us our sins and to cleanse us from all unrighteousness" (1 John 1:9).

Our Relationship with God

Say: "When God forgives you, he is delighted to begin a very special friendship with you. He makes you his child—a member of his family who believes in Jesus. God's Word, the Bible, says . . ."

"But to all who have received him—those who believe in your name—he has given the right to become God's children" (John 1:12 NET).

Say: "Are you ready to ask Jesus to forgive your sins and to be his friend forever? If so, then pray these words after me":

Salvation Prayer

"Dear Jesus, I know I do things I shouldn't do and that these things separate me from you. Please forgive me for my sins. Thank you for dying on the cross for me to pay the price for my sins. Right now, I invite you to come into my life as Lord and Savior. I want to be what you want me to be and to do what you want me to do. Amen."

Assurance of Salvation

Say: "Now as part of God's family you can talk to him every day and be his friend forever."

"Now we can rejoice in our wonderful new relationship with God because our Lord Jesus Christ has made us friends of God" (Rom. 5:11 NLT).

"I give them eternal life, and they will never perish. No one can snatch them away from me" (John 10:28 NLT).

Salvation is a supernatural work of God. You are not responsible for the salvation of any person—including your child. But you *are* responsible for tilling the soil of their heart and sharing the seeds of truth about the Savior. As you plant seeds, pray that the soil of your child's heart will be fertile and receive the seed and that it will take root and bear fruit.

About the Author

One of the world's leading biblical counselors, June Hunt is also an author, speaker, singer, and the founder of HOPE FOR THE HEART, a worldwide biblical counseling ministry. June hosts an award-winning radio broadcast, HOPE FOR THE HEART, heard daily across America. In addition, HOPE IN THE NIGHT is June's live two-hour call-in counseling program that helps people untangle their problems with biblical hope and practical help. HOPE FOR THE HEART'S radio broadcasts air daily on over 350 stations nationwide.

Early family pain was the catalyst that shaped June's compassionate heart. Later, as a youth director for more than six hundred teenagers at a Texas megachurch, she became aware of the need for sound biblical counseling. Her work with young people and their parents led June to a life commitment of providing God's Truth for Today's Problems.

After years of teaching and research, June began developing scripturally based counseling tools called Biblical Counseling Keys that address definitions, characteristics, causes, and steps to solutions for a hundred topics (such as marriage and parenting, anger and abuse, guilt and grief). These one hundred individual topics have been compiled to create the landmark Biblical Counseling Library.

The Counseling Keys have become the foundation for HOPE FOR THE HEART'S Biblical Counseling Institute, initiated by The Criswell College in 2002. Each monthly conference provides training to help spiritual leaders, counselors, and other caring Christians meet the very real needs of others.

June has served as a guest professor at colleges and seminaries, both nationally and internationally, teaching on topics such as crisis counseling, child abuse, domestic violence, depression, alcohol and drug abuse, forgiveness, singleness, and self-worth. The ministry's resources are currently available in more than sixty countries and thirty languages, including Russian, Romanian, Spanish, German, Mandarin, Korean, Japanese, Indonesian, Tamil, Farsi, and Arabic.

June's books have sold more than a million copies and include *Bonding with Your Teen through Boundaries, Caring for a Loved One with Cancer, Hope for Your Heart, the Counseling through Your Bible Handbook, The Answer to Anger, Seeing Yourself through God's Eyes, How to Forgive. . . . When You Don't Feel Like It, How to Handle Your Emotions, How to Rise above Abuse, How to Deal with Difficult Relationships,* and *The Biblical Counseling Reference Guide* (a concordance). Her *Biblical Counseling Keys* have been adapted into a popular minibook series featuring forty-two titles. June is also a contributor to *The Soul Care Bible*, the *Women's Devotional Bible,* and the *NIV Devotional Bible for the Single Woman.* In addition, she provides periodic counseling columns for *The Christian Post.*

June's work has earned numerous accolades, including the 2012 Advanced Writers and Speakers Association's Golden Scroll Lifetime Achievement Award, the 2011 American Association of Christian Counselors' Caregiver Award for lifetime achievement, Christian Women in Media's 2008 Excellence in Communications Award, and the 2008 Lilly Reintegration Award for helping those battling mental illness, and their caregivers.

In all she does, June Hunt is dedicated to presenting *God's Truth for Today's Problems.* Through her life-transforming approach, she readily shares the truth that a *"changed mind* produces a *changed heart . . .* and a *changed heart* produces a *changed life."*

Learn more about June and HOPE FOR THE HEART at:
www.HopeForTheHeart.org
The Hope Center
2001 W. Plano Parkway, Suite 1000
Plano, TX 75075
800-488-HOPE (4673)

Notes

Chapter 1: More than Ever, Your Child Needs Boundaries

1. See June Hunt, *Bonding with Your Teen through Boundaries* (Wheaton, IL: Crossway, 2010), 21.
2. Franklin D. Roosevelt, "Address at University of Pennsylvania," September 20, 1940. See Gerhard Peters and John T. Woolley, *The American Presidency Project*, http://www.presidency.ucsb.edu/wsl?pid=15860/.
3. Daniel Goleman, *Emotional Intelligence* (New York: Bantam, 1995), 261–85.
4. James Dobson, *The New Dare to Discipline* (Carol Stream, IL: Tyndale, 1992), 44.
5. Lawrence J. Crabb Jr., *Understanding People: Deep Longings for Relationships*, Ministry Resources Library (Grand Rapids, MI: Zondervan, 1987), 15–16; Robert S. McGee, *The Search for Significance*, 2nd ed. (Houston, TX: Rapha, 1990), 27–30.
6. James Lehman, *The Total Transformation Program* DVD series (Westbrook, ME: Legacy Parenting Company, 2004).
7. Hunt, *Bonding with Your Teen*, 32.

Chapter 2: What Color Is Your Hat?

1. June Hunt, *Bonding with Your Teen through Boundaries* (Wheaton, IL: Crossway, 2010), 19–24.

Chapter 3: The Confident Parent

1. For this section see June Hunt, *Parenting: Steps for Successful Parenting*, Biblical Counseling Keys Library (Dallas: Hope for the Heart, 2008), 25–28.
2. Josh McDowell, *Why True Love Waits: A Definitive Book on How to Help Your Youth Resist Sexual Pressure* (Wheaton, IL: Tyndale, 2002), 158.
3. For more on this topic, see June Hunt, *Verbal and Emotional Abuse: Victory over Verbal and Emotional Abuse*, Biblical Counseling Keys Library (Dallas: Hope for the Heart, 2008).
4. James Lehman, *The Total Transformation Program* DVD series (Westbrook, ME: Legacy Parenting Company, 2004).
5. For this section see June Hunt, *Confrontation: Challenging Others to*

Change, Biblical Counseling Keys Library (Dallas: Hope for the Heart, 2008), 28–29.
6. For this section see Hunt, *Parenting*.

Chapter 4: Your R & R Toolkit

1. Ken Blanchard, *The One Minute Manager* (New York: William Morrow, 1982), 36.
2. For the difference between task- and time-oriented repercussions, see James Lehman, "How to Give Kids Consequences That Work," *Empowering Parents*, accessed June 27, 2014, http://www.empoweringparents.com /How-to-Give-Kids-Consequences-That-Work.php.
3. James Dobson, *The New Dare to Discipline* (Carol Stream, IL: Tyndale, 1992), 65.
4. Ibid., 72.
5. "Corporal Punishment Policies around the World," *CNN.com*, November 9, 2011, http://www.cnn.com/2011/WORLD/asiapcf/11/08/country .comparisons.corporal.punishment/.
6. Delaware Senate Bill 234, "An Act to Amend Title 11 of the Delaware Code Relating to Offenses against Children," sponsored by Sen. Patricia Blevins, http://www.legis.delaware.gov/LIS/lis146.nsf/vwLegislation/SB+ 234/$file/legis.html?open, accessed January 16, 2015. This bill was enacted on September 12, 2012.
7. James Lehman, "How to Give Kids Consequences."

Chapter 5: Questions and Answers about Boundaries

1. Inspired by Erma Bombeck, *Forever Erma: Best-Loved Writing from America's Favorite Humorist* (Kansas City, MO: Andrews McMeel Universal, 1997), 44–45.
2. June Hunt, *Bonding with Your Teen through Boundaries* (Wheaton, IL: Crossway, 2010), 17.
3. Ibid., 33.
4. James Dobson, *The New Dare to Discipline* (Wheaton, IL: Tyndale, 1992), 39.
5. See Hunt, *Bonding with Your Teen*.
6. Ibid., 34–35.
7. Ibid., 36.
8. Ibid., 23.

Chapter 6: Anger and Aggression

1. See June Hunt, *Anger: Facing the Fire Within*, Biblical Counseling Keys Library (Dallas: Hope for the Heart, 2011).
2. Tara Tegard, "Lessons on the Armor of God: 'How to Win against Sin,'" Ministry-To-Children, accessed June 27, 2014, http://ministry-to-children .com/win-against-sin/.
3. E. M. Cummings, C. D. Kouros, L. M. Papp, "Marital Aggression and Children's Responses to Everyday Inter-Parental Conflict," *European Psychologist* 12, no. 1 (2007): 17–28.

4. Mayo Clinic Staff, "Oppositional Defiant Disorder (ODD)," Mayo Clinic website, June 30, 2014, http://www.mayoclinic.org/diseases-conditions /oppositional-defiant-disorder/basics/definition/con-20024559.

Chapter 8: Bedtime Battles

1. Michelle Trudeau, "Why a Regular Bedtime Is Important for Children," *NPR Health* online, December 16, 2013, www.npr.org/2013/12/16/2514 62015/why-a-regular-bedtime-is-important-for-children.
2. Ibid.

Chapter 10: Bullying

1. Portions of this chapter were adapted from June Hunt, *Bonding with Your Teen through Boundaries* (Wheaton, IL: Crossway, 2010), 119–23.
2. Barbara Coloroso, *The Bully, the Bullied, and the Bystander* (New York: HarperResource, 2003), 13.
3. Ibid., 13–14.
4. CBSNews.com Staff, "Students Say Violence Is Fact of Life," *CBSNews. com*, March 8, 2001, at http://www.cbsnews.com/news/students-say -violence-is-fact-of-life/.
5. "Stop Bullying on the Spot," StopBullying.gov, accessed June 27, 2014, http://www.stopbullying.gov/respond/on-the-spot/index.html.

Chapter 11: Car Etiquette

1. "Time-Out Guidelines for Parents," *Parenting.org*, http://www.parenting .org/article/time-out-guidelines-for-parents, accessed January 16, 2015. This article is adapted from *Help! There's a Toddler in the House* by Thomas M. Reimers (Boys Town, NE: Boys Town Press, 2011).

Chapter 12: Cell Phone Struggles

1. "MRI American Kids Study 2009," *Mediamark Research and Intelligence*, January 4, 2010, http://www.gfkmri.com/PDF/MRIPR_010410_KidsAnd CellPhones.pdf.
2. "Generation M2: Media in the Lives of 8–18 Year Olds," Kaiser Family Foundation online, January 20, 2010, http://www.kff.org/entmedia/mh012 010pkg.cfm.
3. Jessica Ringrose, Rosalind Gill, Sonia Livingstone, and Laura Harvey, "A Qualitative Study of Children and Young People and 'Sexting,'" Joint study of the Institute of Education, London; King's College London; London School of Economics and Political Science, and Open University, 2012, http://www.lse.ac.uk/media@lse/documents/MPP/Sexting-Report -NSPCC.pdf.

Chapter 13: Cheating

1. Brian D. Bloomfield, "The Honorable Thing to Do: A Survey and Analysis of Honor Codes and Councils in DC Independent Schools" (undated), The School for Ethical Education, accessed June 28, 2014, http://ethicsed.org /files/documents/bloomfield.pdf.

Chapter 14: Chores

1. PeggySue Wells, *Rediscovering Your Happily Ever After* (Grand Rapids, MI: Kregel, 2010), 109.

Chapter 15: Cliques

1. *Merriam-Webster Online Dictionary*, s.v. "clique," http://www.merriam -webster.com/dictionary/clique.
2. Kimberly L. Keith, "Children's Cliques," About.com, accessed June 30, 2014, http://childparenting.about.com/od/emotionaldevelopment/a/cliques .htm.

Chapter 17: Disrespectfulness

1. Lisa Welchel, "Controlling the Tongue," Focus on the Family, http://www .focusonthefamily.com/parenting/effective-biblical-discipline/creative -discipline-ideas/controlling-the-tongue. Accessed 1/12/15.
2. Ibid.
3. Kevin Leman, *Have a New Kid by Friday* (Grand Rapids, MI: Revell, 2008), 143–45.

Chapter 18: Disrupting Class

1. "Attention-Deficit/Hyperactivity Disorder," National Institute of Mental Health website, rev. 2012, http://www.nimh.nih.gov/health/publications /attention-deficit-hyperactivity-disorder/index.shtml?utm_source=REFER ENCES_R7#pub2.
2. Ibid.

Chapter 19: Forgetfulness

1. "Baby Brains: A Webinar about Early Childhood Brain Development," Nebraska Children and Families Foundation website, January 27, 2014, http://blog.nebraskachildren.org/tag/brain-development/.
2. "Symptoms and Causes," CHADD (Children and Adults with Attention-Deficit/Hyperactivity Disorder) website, accessed June 28, 2014, http:// www.chadd.org/Understanding-ADHD/Parents-Caregivers-of-Children -with-ADHD/Symptoms-and-Causes.aspx.
3. "Attention-Deficit/Hyperactivity Disorder," National Institute of Mental Health website, rev. 2012, http://www.nimh.nih.gov/health/publications /attention-deficit-hyperactivity-disorder/index.shtml?utm_source=REFER ENCES_R7#pub2.

Chapter 20: Gossip and Tattling

1. Jody Capehart with Emily Hunter and Angela Carnathan, *The New Christian Charm Course: Teacher Book* (Eugene, OR: Harvest House, 2009), 99–100.

Chapter 21: Harmful Habits and Addictions

1. Mark Hyman, "5 Clues You Are Addicted to Sugar," *The Huffington Post*, June 26, 2013, http://www.huffingtonpost.com/dr-mark-hyman/sugar -addiction_b_3502807.html.
2. Sarah Whyte, "Screen-Addicted Children May Have Newest Mental Ill-

ness," *The Sydney Morning Herald* online, October 5, 2012, http://www
.smh.com.au/technology/technology-news/screenaddicted-children-may
-have-newest-mental-illness-20120929-26s7q.html#ixzz2Hjbp2jrv.
3. Vicki Panaccione, "Top Warning Signs of Video Game Addiction," *Parenting Today's Kids*, April 10, 2012, http://parentingtodayskids.com/article
/top-warning-signs-of-video-game-addiction/.
4. Martin Fackler, "In Korea, a Boot Camp Cure for Web Obsession," *The New York Times* online, November 18, 2007, http://www.nytimes.com
/2007/11/18/technology/18rehab.html?pagewanted=all&_r=0/; Julian
Ryall "Japan to Introduce Internet 'Fasting Camps' for Addicted Kids,"
The Telegraph online, http://www.telegraph.co.uk/news/worldnews/asia
/japan/10267303/Japan-to-introduce-internet-fasting-camps-for-addicted
-kids.html/; Michael Moss, "The Extraordinary Science of Addictive Junk
Food," *The New York Times Magazine* online, February 20, 2013, http://
www.nytimes.com/2013/02/24/magazine/the-extraordinary-science-of
-junk-food.html?pagewanted=2/.
5. The Shane Nutrition Staff, "Weight Loss Camps Can Decrease Food Addiction," *Camp Shane* (blog), June 7, 2013, http://campshane.com/blog
/weight-loss-camps-can-decrease-food-addiction/.

Chapter 22: Homework Hassles

1. Walter Burke Barbe, Raymond H. Swassing, and Michael N. Milone Jr.,
Teaching through Modality Strengths: Concepts and Practices (Columbus,
OH: Zaner-Blosner, 1979).

Chapter 23: Interrupting

1. Ellen Galinsky, *Mind in the Making: The Seven Essential Life Skills Every
Child Needs* (New York: HarperCollins, 2010), 63–66; "What's the
Marshmallow Test, and How Does It Predict a Person's Success?" *Discovery Fit and Health* website, 2011, http://curiosity.discovery.com/question
/marshmallow-test-success-prediction; Yuichi Shoda, Walter Mischel, and
Philip K. Peake, "Predicting Adolescent Cognitive and Self-Regulatory
Competencies from Preschool Delay of Gratification: Identifying Diagnostic Conditions," *Developmental Psychology* online 26, no. 6 (1990):
978–86, http://www.webcitation.org/62C0yfhcJ.

Chapter 24: Lying

1. Ellen Booth Church, "Ages and Stages: Honesty: 5 to 6 I'm Not Lying,"
Early Childhood Today online, accessed January 22, 2015, http://www
.scholastic.com/teachers/article/ages-stages-honesty.
2. June Hunt, *Counseling through Your Bible Handbook* (Eugene, OR: Harvest House, 2008), 242.
3. June Hunt, *Lying: How to Stop Truth Decay*, Biblical Counseling Keys
Library (Dallas: Hope for the Heart, 2008), 2.
4. Kevin Leman, *Have a New Kid by Friday* (Grand Rapids, MI: Revell,
2008), 184–85.

5. *Oxford Dictionaries* Language Matters online, s.v. "truth," 2014, http://www.oxforddictionaries.com/us/definition/english/truth#truth__16.

Chapter 25: Mealtime Tussles

1. Jim Daly, "Dinner: Nourish Your Family . . . As a Family," *Focus on the Family.com*, December 1, 2012, http://www.focusonthefamily.com/parenting/parenting_roles/dads_make-every-day-count/dinner-nourish-your-family-as-a-family.aspx.
2. Elsevier Health Sciences, "Families Are 'Lovin' It': Parents' Work Influences How Often Family Meals Are Eaten Outside of Home" *ScienceDaily*, May 7, 2011, http://www.sciencedaily.com/releases/2011/05/110506073825.htm.
3. Elsevier Health Sciences, "Children Eating More, and More Frequently Outside the Home," *ScienceDaily*, July 25, 2011, http://www.sciencedaily.com/releases/2011/07/110725091709.htm.
4. David Sack, "Kids on Sweets: Are We Raising A Generation of Sugar Addicts?" *The Huffington Post*, September 6, 2013, http://www.huffingtonpost.com/david-sack-md/kids-sugar_b_3862244.html.
5. "Food Allergy and Intolerance," *Better Health Channel*, accessed January 22, 2015, http://www.betterhealth.vic.gov.au/bhcv2/bhcarticles.nsf/pages/food_allergy_and_intolerance/; Ashley Miller, "Signs and Symptoms of Sodium Benzoate Intolerance in Children," Livestrong.com, last updated August 16, 2013, http://www.livestrong.com/article/549742-signs-symptoms-of-sodium-benzoate-intolerance-in-children/.
6. Obesity Prevention Source, "Healthy Weight Checklist," Harvard School of Public Health, http://www.hsph.harvard.edu/obesity-prevention-source/diet-lifestyle-to-prevent-obesity/, accessed January 16, 2015. For more information see, "Eat Healthy," Let's Move, http://www.letsmove.gov/eat-healthy.

Chapter 26: Media Mania

1. David Hinckley, "Americans Spend 34 Hours a Week Watching TV, According to Nielsen numbers," *DailyNews* online, September 19, 2012, http://www.nydailynews.com/entertainment/tv-movies/americans-spend-34-hours-week-watching-tv-nielsen-numbers-article-1.1162285.
2. "Generation M2: Media in the Lives of 8–18 Year Olds," Kaiser Family Foundation online, January 20, 2010, http://www.kff.org/entmedia/mh012010pkg.cfm.
3. "New Research from Common Sense Media Reveals Mobile Media Use Among Young Children Has Tripled in Two Years," Common Sense Media, October 28, 2013, http://www.commonsensemedia.org/about-us/news/press-releases/new-research-from-common-sense-media-reveals-mobile-media-use-among/.
4. M. N. Garrison, K. Liekweg, and D. A. Christakis, "Media Use and Child Sleep: The Impact of Content, Timing, and Environment," *Pediatrics*, 128, no. 1 (2011), 29–35; "Zero to Eight: Children's Media Use in America 2013," *Common Sense Media*, October 28, 2013, http://www.common

sensemedia.org/research/zero-to-eight-childrens-media-use-in-america
-2013/.

5. The National Institute on Media and the Family documented the violent nature of certain videos games in its report to Congress in order to encourage stricter rating standards for games.

6. "Screen-Addicted Children May Have Newest Mental Illness," *The Sydney Morning Herald* online, October 5, 2012, http://www.smh.com.au /technology/technology-news/screenaddicted-children-may-have-newest -mental-illness-20120929-26s7q.html#ixzz2Hjbp2jrv/.

7. Kimberly J. Mitchell, David Finkelhor, Lisa M. Jones, and Janis Wolak, "Prevalence and Characteristics of Youth Sexting: A National Study," *Pediatrics* 129, no. 1 (2012): 13–20.

8. Jessica Ringrose, Rosalind Gill, Sonia Livingstone, and Laura Harvey, "A Qualitative Study of Children and Young People and 'Sexting,'" Joint Study of the Institute of Education, London; King's College London; London School of Economics and Political Science, and Open University (2012), http://www .lse.ac.uk/media@lse/documents/MPP/Sexting-Report-NSPCC.pdf.

9. American Academy of Pediatrics, "Media Use by Children Younger Than 2 Years," *Pediatrics*, 128, no. 5 (2011): 1040–45.

10. "3 Simple Rules for a Healthy Media Diet," *Common Sense Media*, December 29, 2012, http://www.commonsensemedia.org/advice-for-parents /3-simple-rules-for-a-healthy-media-diet.

Chapter 27: Money and Materialism

1. Betsy Brown Braun, "Well Said: Betsy's Favorite Expressions and Phrases," *Betsy Brown*, accessed June 30, 2014, http://betsybrownbraun.com /betsyisms/betsys-favorite-things/.

2. June Hunt, *Bonding with Your Teen through Boundaries* (Wheaton, IL: Crossway, 2010), 145.

Chapter 28: Music Matters

1. Genna Martin, "Frequently Asked Questions," *Dangerous Decibels*, accessed June 30, 2014, http://www.dangerousdecibels.org/education /information-center/faq/#mp3-ages.

Chapter 29: Occult Fascination

1. For more information on this topic, see June Hunt, *The Occult: Demystifying the Deeds of Darkness*, Biblical Counseling Keys Library (Dallas: Hope for the Heart, 2009).

2. James Walker, "What Is the Occult?" in *Watchman Expositor* 9, no. 8 (Arlington, TX: Watchman Fellowship, 1992).

3. Hunt, *The Occult*, 22–24.

Chapter 30: Peer Pressure

1. For information on how kids communicate, see PBS Parents, "Talking with Kids," PBS.org, accessed January 16, 2015, http://www.pbs.org/parents /talkingwithkids/agebyage.html,

2. Adapted from "The TI Ethics Quick Test," Texas Instruments website, ac-

cessed June 30, 2014, http://www.ti.com/corp/docs/company/citizen/ethics
/quicktest.shtml.

Chapter 31: Procrastination

1. For this section, see June Hunt, *Procrastination: Preventing the Decay of Delay*, Biblical Counseling Keys Library (Dallas, TX: Hope for the Heart, 2008).
2. "Writing S.M.A.R.T. Goals," *UHR Employee Development*, undated pdf, University of Virginia Human Resources, accessed June 30, 2014, http://www.hr.virginia.edu/uploads/documents/media/Writing_SMART_Goals.pdf.

Chapter 33: Sexual Curiosity

1. For more information on this topic, see Grace Ketterman, *Teaching Your Child about Sex: An Essential Guide for Parents* (Grand Rapids, MI: Revell, 2007).

Chapter 34: Sexual Storms

1. Danna Gresh, *Six Ways to Keep the "Little" in Your Girl* (Eugene, OR: Harvest House, 2010), 34.
2. APA Task Force, "Sexualization of Girls Is Linked to Common Mental Health Problems in Girls and Women—Eating Disorders, Low Self-Esteem, and Depression," An APA (American Psychological Association) Task Force Report, February 19, 2007, http://www.apa.org/news/press/releases/2007/02/sexualization.aspx.
3. Ibid.
4. Jessica Ringrose, Rosalind Gill, Sonia Livingstone, and Laura Harvey, "A Qualitative Study of Children and Young People and 'Sexting,'" Joint study of the Institute of Education, London; King's College London; London School of Economics and Political Science, and Open University (2012), http://www.lse.ac.uk/media@lse/documents/MPP/Sexting-Report-NSPCC.pdf.
5. For this section, see Vicki Courtney, *Your Boy: Raising a Godly Son in an Ungodly World* (Nashville: BandH, 2006), 111.
6. We recommend Gresh, *Six Ways to Keep the "Little" in Your Girl* as well as Gresh's *Secret Keeper Girl* website, www.secretkeepergirl.com; Jennie Bishop's Purity Works ministry (www.purityworks.org); and Jennifer Strickland's *Girl Perfect* study guide (Lake Mary, FL: Charisma House, 2008).
7. Courtney, *Your Boy*, 111.
8. We recommend Courtney, *Your Boy*; Dennis Rainey, *Aggressive Girls, Clueless Boys: 7 Conversations You Must Have with Your Son: 7 Questions You Should Ask Your Daughter* (Little Rock, AR: Family Life, 2012); and *Passport to Purity Getaway Kit* from Family Life Today, http://shop.familylife.com/p-1988-passport2purity-getaway-kit.aspx/.

Chapter 35: Sibling Rivalry and Selfishness

1. Po Bronson with Ashley Merriman, *Nurture Shock: New Thinking about Children* (New York: Hachette Book Group, 2009), 129–30.
2. Ibid., 127.

Chapter 36: Sportsmanship Spats

1. Michael Austin, "Ethics for Everyone: Moral Wisdom for the Modern World," *Psychology Today* website, July 12, 2010, http://www.psychology today.com/blog/ethics-everyone/201007/winning-isnt-everything.
2. Po Bronson and Ashley Merriman, *NurtureShock: New Thinking about Children* (New York: Hachette Book Group, 2009), 131.
3. Michael Alison Chandler, "In Schools, Self-Esteem Boosting Is Losing Favor to Rigor, Finer-Tuned Praise," *The Washington Post* online, January 15, 2012, http://www.washingtonpost.com/local/education/in-schools -self-esteem-boosting-is-losing-favor-to-rigor-finer-tuned-praise/2012/01 /11/gIQAXFnF1P_story.html/; KifZui Mom, "Seven Ways Over-Praising Children Can Do Harm (And What We Can Say or Do Instead)," Kid-Zui (blog), July 28, 2011, http://blog.kidzui.com/2011/07/over-praising -children/.

Chapter 38: Substance Abuse

1. Center for Disease Control and Prevention, "Alcohol and Public Health," 2011, http://www.cdc.gov/alcohol/fact-sheets/underage-drinking.htm.
2. Paul C. Reisser, *Family, Health, Nutrition, and Fitness* (Carol Stream, IL: Tyndale, 2006), 427–500.
3. See Partnership for Drug-Free Kids website: "Parents have more influence over their child than friends, music, TV, the Internet and celebrities," http:// www.drugfree.org/prevent.
4. For this section, see U.S. Department of Health and Human Services, "Results from the 2010 National Survey on Drug Use and Health: Summary of National Findings," 2010, http://www.samhsa.gov/data/NSDUH/2k10 NSDUH/2k10Results.htm.

Chapter 39: Tardiness

1. "Children and Sleep," National Sleep Foundation website, accessed June 30, 2014, http://sleepfoundation.org/sleep-topics/children-and-sleep.

Chapter 41: Whining

1. Laura Markham, "The Cure for Whining," *Aha! Parenting.com*, 2014, http://www.ahaparenting.com/ages-stages/preschoolers/Life-Preschooler /pre-empt-whining.

Appendix: How to Lead Your Child to Christ

1. Dan Graves, "Jesse Overholter and Child Evangelism," *Christianity.com*, June 2007, http://www.christianity.com/church/church-history/timeline /1901-2000/jesse-overholtzer-and-child-evangelism-11630811.html.

A Biblical Approach to 36 Topics Ranging from
Breaking Curfew to Back Talk to Bullying

"With a 'how-to' practicality, June Hunt helps
parents tackle the hardest problems their
kids face on the road to adulthood."
Josh McDowell, author & speaker

Biblical Hope for the Storms of Life

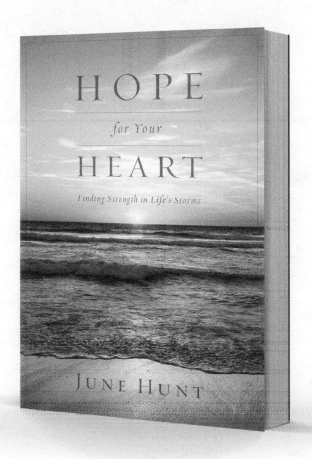

"If your world seems to be spinning out of control into nightmarish chaos, June Hunt shows you where to find stability and safety in her excellent book."
Steve Douglass, President, Campus Crusade for Christ International